GUIDE FOR CELEBRATING™ FIRST COMMUNION

JO-ANN METZDORFF

PAUL TURNER

LITURGY TRAINING PUBLICATIONS

Nihil Obstat
Very Reverend Daniel A. Smilanic, JCD
Vicar for Canonical Services
Archdiocese of Chicago
January 30, 2015

Imprimatur
Very Reverend Ronald A. Hicks
Vicar General
Archdiocese of Chicago
January 30, 2015

The *Nihil Obstat* and *Imprimatur* are declarations that the material is free from doctrinal or moral error, and thus is granted permission to publish in accordance with c. 827. No legal responsibility is assumed by the grant of this permission. No implication is contained herein that those who have granted the *Nihil Obstat* and *Imprimatur* agree with the content, opinions, or statements expressed.

Scripture readings are from the *New American Bible*, revised edition © 2010, 1991, 1986, 1970 Confraternity of Christian Doctrine, Washington, DC. Used with permission. All rights reserved. No part of the New American Bible may be reproduced without permission in writing from the copyright owner.

Excerpts from *Eastern Catholics in the United States of America*, adapted text copyright © 1999, United States Catholic Conference, Inc., Washington, DC. All rights reserved. Excerpts from the *Catechism of the Catholic Church*, second edition, copyright © 2000, Libreria Editrice Vaticana-United States Conference of Catholic Bishops, Inc., Washington, DC. All rights reserved. Excerpts from *Disciples Called to Witness: The New Evangelization* copyright © 2012, United States Conference of Catholic Bishops, Washington, DC. All rights reserved. Excerpts from *National Directory for Catechesis* copyright © 2005, United States Conference of Catholic Bishops, Washington, DC. All rights reserved. Excerpts from *National Statutes for the Catechumenate* copyright © 1988, United States Catholic Conference, Inc., Washington, DC. All rights reserved. Excerpts from *Built of Living Stones: Art, Architecture, and Worship* copyright © 2000, United States Catholic Conference, Inc., Washington, DC. All rights reserved. Excerpts from *Sing to the Lord: Music in Divine Worship* copyright © 2007, United States Conference of Catholic Bishops, Washington, DC. All rights reserved.

Excerpts from the English translation of *Directory for Masses with Children* © 1973, International Commission on English in the Liturgy Corporation (ICEL); excerpts from the English translation of *Eucharistic Prayers for Masses with Children* © 1975, ICEL; excerpts from *Documents on the Liturgy, 1963–1979: Conciliar, Papal, and Curial Texts* © 1982, ICEL; excerpts from the English translation of *Rite of Christian Initiation of Adults* © 1985, ICEL; excerpts from the English translation of *The Roman Missal* © 2010, ICEL. All rights reserved. Texts contained in this work derived whole or in part from liturgical texts copyrighted by the International Commission on English in the Liturgy (ICEL) have been published here with the confirmation of the Committee on Divine Worship, United States Conference of Catholic Bishops. No other texts in this work have been formally reviewed or approved by the United States Conference of Catholic Bishops.

The glossary was compiled from material written by Jennifer Kerr Breedlove, Joseph DeGrocco, Corinna Laughlin, Dennis Smolarski, and Kenneth A. Riley © Liturgy Training Publications. Additional material prepared by Jennifer Kerr Breedlove (Order of Mass/music) and Dr. Mary Ehle, PHD (celiac disease) © Liturgy Training Publications.

Photo on p. 9 courtesy the Sacred Heart Parish Archives (Winnetka, Illinois). Photo on p. 22 © Irene Sanchez. All other photos © John Zich. Art on p. v by Kathy Ann Sullivan ©LTP.

Preparing Parish Worship™: Guide for Celebrating™ First Communion © 2015 Archdiocese of Chicago: Liturgy Training Publications, 3949 South Racine Avenue, Chicago, IL 60609, 1-800-933-1800; fax 1-800-933-7094; e-mail: orders@ltp.org. All rights reserved. See our website at www.LTP.org.

19 18 17 16 15   1 2 3 4 5

Printed in the United States of America.

Library of Congress Control Number: 2015932687

ISBN 978-1-61671-235-8

EGCFC

CONTENTS

PREFACE iv

WELCOME 1

Theological and Historical Overview of
First Communion   4

Preparing the First Communion Liturgy   22

Frequently Asked Questions   78

APPENDIX I: The Sacrament of Reconciliation   95

APPENDIX II: Other Ritual Experiences for Children   101

RESOURCES 111

GLOSSARY 115

PREFACE

Anna walked into the house and saw dough rising. Nothing unusual about that. Her mother baked some of the best bread in the community. But it was unusual to see so much dough. Not just one loaf for the family to eat today. But three, four, maybe half a dozen balls of dough rising in the sunshine.

Anna ran to the stream where her mother had gone to draw water. "Mother, is there going to be a party? Will there be singing and dancing?" Phoebe smiled. "Not exactly, dear. But your father and I have decided to invite some of our neighbors tonight."

"They're all coming to our house?" Anna had tagged along this week while her parents went from home to home for long meetings every evening. She did not understand everything. Some people sang songs. Others told stories. Still others reported news about their neighbors, especially those in trouble.

"Are we going to get all wet again?" Anna giggled. Yesterday, Anna watched while someone took her parents to the stream and plunged them underwater three times. It looked fun, so she did not object when her parents helped them bring Anna into the water too.

"No, Anna. That was the only time that will happen. But we are all becoming closer with these friends. This morning, Stachys brought over extra grain. We don't have enough money to buy this much. He has more, so he shared."

"I shared my dogs with Berta."

"Yes, you did, honey. That was nice."

The aroma of freshly-baked bread filled the house as the community gathered that evening. Laughter echoed around the room as friends greeted friends with loving compassion and good news.

"Did you hear about Junia?" Aquila could hardly wait to ask Phoebe. "She's been healed!"

"Healed! Praise God!"

"Linus prayed over her, placed his hands on her head, anointed her with oil, and we could see strength returning to her body!"

Junia had been one of the first to hear the news about Jesus, the one called the Christ. She learned from other women how he had lived a good life, worked wonders, and gathered followers. But he was arrested and put to death on a cross "because he got too popular," Junia always said when she got to this part of the story. "Wish I could have been there," she always said.

Junia's strong presence could win arguments and disciples. But in recent weeks, her health had failed, and only a miracle, it seemed, would save her. Now this. Healed!

As the evening progressed, people divided up responsibilities. Some would watch children while others spread the word about Jesus to new groups. Some would listen to the leaders and learn more about the works of Jesus and the words of his Apostles. Still others would visit members of the community to learn who had needs, and who had the means to help.

"No one should suffer here," said Aquila. "If anyone learns that someone is sick, too poor to eat, or without sufficient clothing, we want to know."

Anna listened to all of this politely and with interest, but something else kept distracting her: the smell of bread.

Finally, the group sat down while one of the men said prayers and told another story about Jesus. Then he picked up the loaves of bread, broke them, and shared them with those who had gathered.

"I want some," said Anna. Phoebe paused a moment. "I want you to have some, dear, but this is not ordinary bread."

Anna looked puzzled. It sure looked like bread. It looked exactly like the ordinary bread she ate each day. Her mother said, "You eat this bread on one condition." Anna was expecting the usual kind of request: Sweep the house. Feed the dogs. Wash the dishes. But she heard something else.

"You must follow Jesus and help us tell others about him too. Will you do that?"

Anna looked around the room at the dozens of people who smiled and laughed, sang and prayed. She wanted more of this, a lifetime of this. "Yes, Mother."

She ate bread and drank wine with them for the first time.

"They devoted themselves to the teaching of the apostles and to the communal life, to the breaking of the bread and to the prayers. Awe came upon everyone, and many wonders and signs were done through the apostles. All who believed were together and had all things in common; they would sell their property and possessions and divide them among all according to each one's need. Every day they devoted themselves to meeting together in the temple area and to breaking bread in their homes. They ate their meals with exultation and sincerity of heart, praising God and enjoying favor with all the people. And every day the Lord added to their number those who were being saved."[1]

—Paul Turner

---

[1] Acts of the Apostles 2:42–47.

WELCOME

First Communion happens only once in a lifetime. Joy fills the air as children anticipate the day.

For all their lives thus far, they have watched other people receive Communion. After hearing "Blessed are those called to the supper of the Lamb" at every Mass, they scooched over so that parents and older siblings could gain access to the aisle. Or the children came forward with others and walked toward the altar, where they stood and watched others proclaim their faith and extend their hands or open their mouths. In younger years these same children may have reached for the host, informing the minister, "I want one." In later years they remained obedient, but they grew more and more hungry.

All that changes with First Communion. At a basic human level, a child will feel included. On the spiritual level, the child will enjoy union with Jesus Christ and with his Body the Church.

Children may have witnessed their older siblings and friends celebrate their own First Communion. They have seen the ceremony, the formal attire, the photography, and the gifts. They know that Communion on any day is important, but one's First Communion puts a child at the center of attention. They have been waiting, and now they have matured enough to take their place in procession and acclaim "Amen" with a smile.

Parents, too, have anticipated the First Communion of their children. On the day that children are baptized, their parents promise to bring them up according to the law of Christ and the Church. They now deliver on that promise in a special way. They have guided their children through the first years of faith, teaching them the importance of prayer and catechesis, as well as the need to live as Christians do. They have taught repentance and forgiveness, unity and charity. Children have developed an interior spiritual life. Parents have experienced the rewards of sharing the Gospel with others.

As the big day draws near, the entire community wants to celebrate well. Much is at stake. First Communion imprints a memory on virtually every Catholic child. Parents, priests, deacons, catechists, liturgists and music ministers, family and friends all want a successful day that will comfort the child in years to come and create stories that can be joyfully repeated from one generation to the next.

About This Book

This book aims to help those responsible for parish liturgies prepare and celebrate First Communion Masses. It will offer ideas for preparing well-crafted and beautiful parish First Communion liturgies. You will find a glossary of terms that you may find unfamiliar. You will also learn about resources for additional information about the Mass, the liturgy, and preparing the Masses for First Communion.

You will learn the story of how the Catholic Church started celebrating First Communion, and you'll see how the story of today's children seamlessly fits into that narrative. This book will address practical matters of all types, from the sublime meaning of Communion in the Catholic Church to the ordinary concerns of photography. And, of course, the dress.

Welcome to *Preparing Parish Worship*™: *Guide for Celebrating*™ *First Communion*. Some children you know are now bursting with excitement over an upcoming once-in-a-lifetime event. May you find here the ideas, the answers, and the strength you seek to grasp those children by the hand and lead them in faith toward the bountiful table of the Lord.[1]

About the Authors

Jo-Ann Metzdorff is the director of religious education and RCIA at the parish of St. Agnes Cathedral in Rockville Centre, New York. She holds a bachelor's degree in art education from St. John's University, New York, a master's in elementary education from Adelphi University, and master's degrees in theology from the Seminary of the Immaculate Conception, New York, and the University of Notre Dame. Her doctor of ministry degree is from the Seminary of the Immaculate Conception. Dr. Metzdorff provided

---

[1] *Guide for Celebrating*™ *First Communion* is part of the *Preparing Parish Worship*™ series. This resource should not replace the diocesan approved curriculum for First Communion catechesis and formation. *Guide for Celebrating*™ *First Communion* is not meant to help parish staffs teach children about the Eucharist and their participation in the liturgy but rather it is designed to help parish staffs prepare beautiful and appropriate First Communion liturgies.

the "Theological Formation for First Communion," "Preparing for the First Communion Liturgy," "Frequently Asked Questions," and "Resources."

Paul Turner is pastor of St. Anthony Parish in Kansas City, Missouri. A priest of the Diocese of Kansas City-St. Joseph, he holds a doctorate in sacred theology from Sant' Anselmo in Rome. His publications include *At the Supper of the Lamb* (Chicago: Liturgy Training Publications, 2011); *Glory in the Cross* (Collegeville: Liturgical Press, 2011); *ML Bulletin Inserts* (San Jose: Resource Publications, 2012); and *Celebrating Initiation: A Guide for Priests* (Chicago: World Library Publications, 2008). He is a former president of the North American Academy of Liturgy, and a member of Societas Liturgica and the Catholic Academy of Liturgy. He is the 2013 recipient of the Jubilate Deo Award (National Association of Pastoral Musicians) and the Frederick McManus Award (Federation of Diocesan Liturgical Commissions). He serves as a facilitator for the International Commission on English in the Liturgy. Fr. Turner has provided the "Preface," "Welcome," and "History of the Ritual of First Communion."

Theological and Historical Overview of First Communion

> "The Eucharist is the ritual, sacramental action of giving thanks and praise to the Father. It is the sacrificial memorial of Christ in his word and in his Spirit."
>
> —*National Directory for Catechesis*, 36 A 3

Although this resource is primarily for preparing the First Communion liturgy, those who work with children and prepare the First Communion Mass should have a theological understanding of the liturgy and of the Eucharist. Preparation for the First Communion liturgy begins long before a child starts formal religious instruction. It begins at home, in the family—the Domestic Church.[1] At Baptism, parents promise to be the first teachers of the faith for their children.[2] Preparation begins here, at the beginning of a child's life in Christ, in simple steps, and continues in the family even as they attend formal classes. This preparation at home is not complicated. Parents are preparing their children to receive Communion when they show their children what it means to love as Christ loves, to pray, to make little sacrifices for others, to go to Mass, to ask forgiveness, and to be in relationship with Christ. This can begin from the time a child becomes aware of his

Preparation for First Communion begins at Baptism.

---

1 This section on the formation of children should not replace the First Communion curriculum approved for use in your diocese or archdiocese.

2 See *Rite of Baptism*, 39.

or her surroundings and the people who care for them. Parents should take every opportunity to pray with their children, to read Bible stories, to answer children's questions about God, and to familiarize their children with the Catholic faith. Children have a great capacity to connect with God, and for those who grow up in a faith-filled household that will be evident as they grow and mature. It will also affect the way they perceive and respond to formal religious education. The parents' responsibility does not end when their children begin preparing for First Communion and Reconciliation with formal catechesis. The parish assists the parents, but their part in the formation of their children is essential for the child to be ready to receive Communion and grow in their faith life.

> It is primarily the duty of parents and those who take the place of parents, as well as the duty of pastors, to take care that children who have reached the use of reason are prepared properly and, after they have made sacramental confession, are refreshed with this divine food as soon as possible. It is for the pastor to exercise vigilance so that children who have not attained the use of reason or whom he judges are not sufficiently disposed do not approach holy communion.
>
> — *Code of Canon Law*, 914

Catechesis for Eucharist is a lifelong process of coming to understand what the Eucharist is, how it relates to our lives as Catholic Christians, and what the Eucharist calls us to become. The *National Directory for Catechesis* outlines what an adequate catechesis for Eucharist should include. This catechesis is so important that it includes catechesis on the Eucharist for adults as well as children.

> Parents also have the right and the duty to be involved in preparing their children for First Communion. The catechesis offered should help parents grow in their own understanding and appreciation of the Eucharist and enable them to catechize their children more effectively.[3]

While it is important that all adult Catholics have a well-formed understanding of the Eucharist, it is essential that those responsible for catechizing and forming children for the sacrament not only have an understanding of the Eucharist, but also a well-formed Eucharistic spirituality and devotion. In this way, they can impart to the children a love for the Eucharist and a great desire to receive Christ. Those who work with children need to be

---

3 *National Directory for Catechesis*, 36 A 3a.

especially well prepared. They need to know what the Church teaches regarding the Sacrament of the Eucharist, but they also need to be formed as Eucharistic people so as to impart their love of Christ and his gift of himself to those they are catechizing. The enthusiasm and love they show for the Eucharist then passes on to those children in their charge.

When exploring the meaning of the Eucharist, it goes beyond just receiving the consecrated host at Mass. The Eucharist is not something we get; it is not a thing. The Eucharist is a sacrament of the Church. Sacraments are conduits of God's grace. Grace is a free gift. It is a *"participation in the life of God."*[4] Sacraments are actions that manifest God working in our lives. Part of the preparation of both children and their parents is to help foster in them not only a love of the Eucharist but also a love for the celebration of the Church's liturgy, the Mass. The Church describes the liturgy as "the source and summit of the christian life."[5] As such, a sufficient understanding of the Mass and our participatory role in the Eucharistic celebration is essential.

> The administration of the Most Holy Eucharist to children requires that they have sufficient knowledge and careful preparation so that they understand the mystery of Christ according to their capacity and are able to receive the body of Christ with faith and devotion.
> —*Code of Canon Law*, 913, § 1

As people of hope, we need to believe that what we do to help them to grow in their faith—and to appreciate the Mass and the Eucharist—will be a seed that someday will grow. We need to encourage parents to attend Mass with their children. Often a personal invitation or encouragement from other parents helps. Making sure liturgy is done well in our parishes is essential, as well as creating a sense of hospitality and welcome. This, paired with good catechesis, helps to bring people back to the Mass.

The formation of children differs from that of adults in that it is to be suited to their age and their abilities to comprehend doctrines and concepts concerning the Eucharist. The *National Directory for Catechesis* lists nine points that are basic prerequisites in the preparation of children for the sacrament. These points are also part of an adequate catechesis for parents on the Eucharist.

---

[4] *Catechism of the Catholic Church*, 1997; emphasis in original.
[5] *Lumen gentium*, 11; see also *Constitution on the Sacred Liturgy*, 14.

- The Eucharist is the living memorial of Christ's sacrifice for the salvation of all and the commemoration of his last meal with his disciples
- Teach[] not only "the truths of faith regarding the Eucharist but also how from First Communion on . . . they can as full members of Christ's Body take part actively with the People of God in the Eucharist, sharing in the Lord's table and the community of their brothers and sisters"*
- Ensure[] that the baptized have been prepared, according to their capacity, for the Sacrament of Penance prior to their First Communion
- Develop[] in children an understanding of the Father's love, of their participation in the sacrifice of Christ, and of the gift of the Holy Spirit
- Teach[] "The Holy Eucharist is His real Body and Blood of Christ" and that "what appear to be bread and wine are actually His living body"**
- Teach[] the difference between the Eucharist and ordinary bread
- Teach[] the meaning of reception of the Holy Eucharist under both species of bread and wine
- Help[] children to participate actively and consciously in the Mass
- Help[] children to receive Christ's Body and Blood in an informed and reverent manner[6]

All of these points will be covered in a diocesan-approved curriculum but not necessarily in the sequence presented above. Many of these points are learned as part of formal catechesis but much of it comes from living out our faith in the family and in the parish. It is important to remember, however, that receiving First Communion is not a reward for having learned the concepts and doctrines listed in the *National Directory for Catechesis*. It is first and foremost about having a relationship with Jesus, and that relationship is heightened by the reception of his Body and Blood in Communion. Catechesis and formation for the Eucharist must emphasize and foster this relationship. It must work to develop children and their parents into true disciples of Jesus. St. Augustine wrote when describing receiving the Eucharist, "Behold what you are, become what you receive."[7] When the priest elevates the consecrated bread and wine we are looking upon the Body and Blood of Christ. When

---

6   See *National Directory for Catechesis*, 36 A 3a. *Citing the Directory for *Masses with Children*, 7.
**Citing the *National Catechetical Directory*, 122.
7   St. Augustine, *On the Nature of the Sacrament of the Eucharist*, Sermon 272.

we approach the minister of Communion and gaze upon the host before receiving it, we are gazing upon our Lord and God. When we receive the Body and Blood of Christ in Communion, we receive Christ into our body. But in reality it is more than that. Upon receiving the Eucharist we become part of the Body of Christ. Being part of the Body of Christ means that we are to live our lives differently. We must strive to live our lives in imitation of Jesus and to enter into a deep relationship with him as our companion, our guide, our Lord, and our God, each and every day. As the children grow older, they will see that as members of the Body of Christ they are to bring Christ to others. The Eucharist they receive at Mass is brought to others by the way they live, how they act toward others, and how they demonstrate the love of Christ to friends, family, and even to strangers. Parents, catechists, liturgists, pastors, and other pastoral staff would do well to model this behavior for children, and encourage them to be Christ-like in age-appropriate ways. Disciples are people who sit at the feet of the Master, who learn from him and follow him in their daily lives. Only then can children and their families become truly Eucharistic people. It is a lifelong process.

> A fully Christian life is inconceivable without participation in the liturgical services in which the faithful, gathered into a single assembly, celebrate the paschal mystery.
>
> —*Directory for Masses with Children*, 8

The History of the Ritual of First Communion

The earliest record of a First Communion ceremony resembling today's practice comes from 1593 in the town of Aumale, France. The local priest, Jacques Gallemant, prepared the children intellectually, spiritually, and emotionally. After a period of daily catechesis, he planned to give them Communion separately from others in the community. Holding the Body of Christ in his hands, he stirred up their emotions until they cried for joy and gasped with love. Then he distributed the Communion they longed to receive.[8]

By 1616 the same custom had appeared in Paris on a day that included an exhortation, Communion at Mass, Vespers that evening, and a procession. By 1628 it appeared in Boinvilliers, where people gathered on the Tuesday

---

8 See Paul Turner, *Ages of Initiation* (Collegeville, MN: The Liturgical Press, 2000), CD chap. 10, sect. 7.

The late Monsignor Hillenbrand (American liturgical reformer) distributing First Communion at a parish in the Archdiocese of Chicago, October 1954.

after Easter for a special Mass, during which the children held a candle. The following Sunday they participated at a Vespers service and received gifts such as religious books, or rosaries and medals for those who could not read. The practice rapidly spread to other countries, such as Germany and Switzerland. By the eighteenth century some children wore white garments as a sign of their faith and repeated for themselves the baptismal promises first made by their godparents.[9]

Children were receiving their First Communion at about the age they entered adolescence. The ceremony affirmed the catechesis they had received and launched them into a mature life as Christians in the Church.

This most Catholic of ceremonies developed completely as a grassroots effort. Priests, catechists, and parents immediately saw its value, and they spread the details of the celebration by word of mouth from city to city and country to country. The Vatican never issued an official ceremony of First Communion, and still has not. Consequently, the customs and procedures continue to enjoy some variations from one place to another.

Prior to the turn of the seventeenth century, then, there was no First Communion ceremony as people envision it today. The practice of receiving Communion for the first time went through several stages.

---

9   See *Ages of Initiation*, CD chap. 10, sect. 7.

In the New Testament, there is no record of people sharing Communion on the same occasion that they were baptized. However, only the baptized could receive Communion, and St. Paul thundered against those who ate the bread and drank the cup of the Lord in an unworthy manner.[10] But participation in the Eucharist for the first time seems to have required nothing more than Baptism.

The New Testament neither affirms nor denies that infants were baptized. However, it is logical to assume that children were included in the household Baptisms of those who lived with Cornelius,[11] Stephanas,[12] Lydia,[13] the jailer of Paul and Silas,[14] and Crispus the synagogue official.[15] Since Baptism was given to the entire household, it would be hard to explain why parents would keep their children from receiving it. Paul spoke about the holiness of the children of believers.[16] He also compared Christian Baptism with Jewish circumcision, a ceremony performed on the eighth day of one's birth.[17] Jesus himself spoke favorably of children. He encouraged people to welcome them, and he regarded them as models for accepting the Kingdom of God.[18] If children were baptized, they were eligible for Communion. Although it cannot be proven from the evidence at hand, it is logical to assume that baptized children shared Communion in the apostolic age. It must have been special the first time they did it, but so was their Baptism.

The Eucharist became part of the baptismal liturgy in the second century. Hence, the earliest records of a First Communion are directly connected to the ceremony of Baptism. On the occasion of one's baptismal initiation, one received Communion for the first time. There was no separate First Communion liturgy. First Communion was an initiation rite because it happened together with Baptism. The age of the candidate did not matter; adults and children alike received Communion when they were baptized. St. Cyprian of Carthage († 258) complained about parents bringing children to the communion of pagan sacrifices instead of the Christian Eucharist.[19]

---

10 See 1 Corinthians 11:27–30.
11 See Acts of the Apostles 10:44–48.
12 See 1 Corinthians 1:16.
13 See Acts of the Apostles 16:14–15.
14 See Acts of the Apostles 19–34.
15 See Acts of the Apostles 18:8.
16 See 1 Corinthians 7:14.
17 See Colossians 2:11–13.
18 See Mark 10:14–15; Matthew 18:3–5 and 19:14–15; Luke 9:48 and 18:16–17.
19 See *Ages of Initiation*, chap. 2, sect. 8.

The *Apostolic Tradition* of the third to fourth century explicitly included among the baptized small children unable to speak for themselves.[20] By the fifth century, St. Augustine knew and approved the practice of infants receiving Communion.[21] St. Augustine had a tremendous influence on many areas of Church belief and practice, so his acceptance of infants receiving Communion provided a support for many centuries.[22] The First Communion would have taken place at the baptismal liturgy, which itself must have been a quite moving experience.

Devotional practices gradually arose in conjunction with the Eucharist. For example, in some locales people were expected to fast before Communion. Evidence for the practice appears in some fourth-century regional councils in North Africa and from the writings of St. Augustine, who hailed from the same region.[23]

From these earliest days, people naturally received Communion in the hand and under both the forms of bread and wine. At the Last Supper, Jesus had invited the disciples to "take," "eat," and "drink." The first Christians surely ate and drank at the Eucharist. with their hands, the way they did at home. In time, spiritual significance was placed on the gestures accompanying Communion. St. Cyril of Jerusalem († 386) asked the faithful to approach the sacrament holding their left hand like a throne for the right, in order to receive the King.[24] A synod in Rouen in 878 took the matter further and forbade giving Communion in the hand to lay people, though traces of the practice remained for a couple of centuries more.[25]

The practice of giving Communion directly into the mouth of the faithful coincided with other historical events. Heresies had arisen denying that Christ was truly present in the bread and wine. As the Church reinforced this belief dearly held by the faithful, people began to feel less worthy to receive Communion, or even to touch it with their hands.

Not long after this, the cup was no longer offered to lay communicants for similar reasons. Eucharistic devotion stirred fears that the cup might be

---

20 See Paul Bradshaw, Maxwell E. Johnson, and Edward L. Phillips, *The Apostolic Tradition: A Commentary*, ed. Harold W. Attridge (Minneapolis, MN: Augsburg Fortress, 2002), p. 112.

21 See *Ages of Initiation*, chap. 3, sect. 9.

22 See *Ages of Initiation*, chap. 5, sect. 4.

23 See Pius XII, "*Christus Dominus*: Concerning the Discipline to Be Observed with Respect to the Eucharistic Fast," accessed September 1, 2014 http://www.ewtn.com/library/papaldoc/p12chdom.htm.

24 Cited in Anscar J. Chupungco, *Handbook for Liturgical Studies III: The Eucharist* (Collegeville, MN: Liturgical Press, 1999), p. 308.

25 See *Handbook for Liturgical Studies III: The Eucharist*, p. 307.

spilled. The Church also taught that Christ was fully present in either the consecrated bread or the consecrated wine. To simplify the practice, then, and to offer people the essentials without the dangers, Communion was administered to the faithful only under the form of bread.[26]

Up to this time, very young children received Communion. Even infants shared in the Eucharist from the day they were baptized. By the eleventh century, however, the practice was changing. Priests in some places baptized without giving Communion to infants in the same ceremony. Several theologians, including the influential twelfth-century canonist Johannes Gratian, argued that Communion was not necessary for children.[27] Consequently, the reception of First Communion began to be deferred.

Throughout this period, the initiation rites were practiced differently. If a bishop presided at them, he administered Baptism, Confirmation, and Communion together at the same occasion, no matter the age of the candidates: infants, children, or adults. When a priest baptized infants, he offered them Communion as well, and the bishop would confirm when he was available. The word "initiation" became associated with whatever rites were performed at Baptism. Whenever a child's First Communion followed some years after Baptism, only Baptism was understood as a Rite of Initiation.[28]

Priests were probably using leavened bread at the Eucharist for the first thousand years or more. This seems true in both Eastern and Western Churches. The Eastern Rites still use leavened bread. The Western Churches do not, but evidence for the use of leaven in the West can be found as late as the eleventh century. Ulrich of Zell († 1093) described the practice of making bread at the monastery at Cluny. One of the monks kneaded the bread vigorously. That would only be required if the bread were leavened.[29] Over the centuries, though, unleavened bread became the universal practice in the Roman Rite.

The practice of sharing Communion with infants, already being questioned in the eleventh century, ceased more universally in the thirteenth. To be specific, in 1215, the Fourth Lateran Council required all those who had reached the age of discretion to confess their sins at least once a year.

---

26 See *Handbook for Liturgical Studies III: The Eucharist*, p. 305.

27 See *Handbook for Liturgical Studies III: The Eucharist*, chap. 7, sect. 5.

28 See Turner, "'Initiation' in Theological Expression," *"Imaginer la théologie catholique", Permanence et transformations de la foi en attendant Jesus-Christ: Melanges offerts a Ghislain Lafont*, ed. Jeremy Driscoll, Studia Anselmiana 129 (Rome: Centro Studi Sant' Anselmo: 2000): pp.487–499.

29 See Barry Craig, *Fractio panis: A History of the Breaking of Bread in the Roman Rite* (Studia Anselmiana. Rome: EOS–Editions of Sankt Ottilien, 2011), p. 181.

It also required people to receive Communion at least once a year during Easter Time.

By this time, devotion to the real presence of Christ in the Eucharist had become so strong, and the faithful were feeling so undeserving, that many of them had refrained from receiving Communion at all. To change this deplorable custom, the Council required the faithful to receive Communion at least once a year during Easter, preceded by confession. The Council Fathers hoped not to discourage Communion, but to promote it.

The law became effective for each individual at "the age of discretion," a term the Council did not define, but rather left open to interpretation. Still, the expression pertained to the confession of sins, which implied that it came at the age when people should be able to determine right from wrong. Several theologians argued that the age of discretion came when a person obtained "the capacity for deception"—that is, the ability to commit a crime or a sin. Various writers placed the age within a range of seven to fourteen.

The Fourth Lateran Council did not forbid giving Communion to those younger than the age of discretion, but in practice that is what happened. Such children were considered ineligible. The Council did not require confession before every Communion, but that is what many believed. Hence, as Communion was withheld from infants, it was offered to the faithful only after they had reached the age of responsibility for sin and had confessed their offenses to their own priest.[30]

In the Eastern Rites, however, no similar change happened. Infants being baptized continued to receive their First Communion at the same occasion. In fact, priests had the faculty to confirm, so newborns received all three Sacraments of Initiation on the same occasion. That longstanding practice continues even today. The initiation practices of East and West dramatically diverged from the thirteenth century on.[31]

By the thirteenth century, theologians such as Alexander of Hales and St. Thomas Aquinas argued that children should receive Communion for the first time around the ages of ten or eleven. Readiness could be measured by their ability to use reason, that is, to distinguish Eucharistic food from ordinary food and to show consequent devotion toward the sacrament. In time, though, the age for First Communion continued to rise further. Some

---

30 See Craig, chap. 8, sect. 5.
31 See Craig, chap. 8, sect. 7.

received Communion as late as age eighteen.[32] The origins of the expressions "age of discretion" and "age of reason" were associated with the Sacraments of Confession and Communion respectively. At this time, the first was thought to precede the second.

After the Protestant Reformation, the Catholic Church of the sixteenth century began requiring more catechetical formation for children.[33] Martin Luther had authored catechisms, and the Catholic Church issued its own landmark catechism in 1566, one of the first fruits of the Council of Trent. With a manual in hand, the Church could gradually demand more unified and extensive formation for children. The deferral of First Communion beyond infancy created a void that preparatory catechesis naturally filled.

All of this laid the background for the idea that Jacques Gallemant brought to Aumale in 1593. Not only would he prepare children for their First Communion, but he would stir up their emotional desire for it. Not only would they understand the real presence of Christ intellectually, they would prepare to receive it devotionally. First Communion ceremonies met a specific need in the Catholic Church of Gallemant's day. They helped the faithful hand on their core beliefs to the next generation.

First Communion ceremonies continued to develop through the nineteenth century. Elements that connected Communion to Baptism appeared. At one church in France, children knelt before the font in which they had been baptized, held candles, and renewed their promises. All the faithful were obliged to receive Communion at least once a year during Easter Time, so First Communion ceremonies were prepared for that season as an aid to children. The whole event must have made a tremendous impression on children who had attained an advanced stage of catechetical progress and stood as a sign of their adulthood in the Church. According to one eye witness, Napoleon Bonaparte, at the height of his fame and glory, when pressed at a banquet one night to name the happiest day of his life, declined to assign it to any of his victorious battles. Instead, he named his First Communion day.[34]

Napoleon would have been an adolescent then. But by the next century, the history of First Communion underwent a significant change again. In 1910 the Sacred Congregation for the Discipline of the Sacraments with the approval of Pope Pius X reestablished the first reception of Communion for

---

32 See Craig, chap. 8, sect. 9.
33 See Craig, chap. 9, sect. 4.
34 See Craig, chap. 10, sect. 7.

children at a younger age.[35] In one sense, they did nothing new. The age of First Communion had risen to adolescence over the previous centuries, but no Vatican document had authorized it. The most recent decree pertaining to the question was from the Fourth Lateran Council of 1215. As indicated above, this Council did not forbid the Communion of infants. However, the practice ceased in the light of the Council's requirement that those above the age of discretion confess their sins once a year. In its 1910 decree *Quam singulari*, the Sacred Congregation said that the age of discretion was the time when one could distinguish right from wrong, and its members equated "age of reason" with "a certain use of reason;" that is, the time when one could distinguish Eucharistic bread from ordinary food. The Congregation placed this around the age of seven, or even younger.[36]

Initially, the change in legislation met a mixed reaction. Certainly there were those rejoicing that young children could now share in Communion. However, the decree posed a difficulty for catechists. They were used to preparing children around the age of twelve. Now their materials were not useful for children of a younger age. The decree was promulgated in August of 1910. By the following Easter Time countless children between the ages of seven and twelve had to be prepared to receive Communion, or risk falling into sin for failing their Easter Communion duty.[37] Nonetheless, people rose to the challenge, and the new system was largely welcomed. The new legislation was codified in the 1917 *Code of Canon Law*,[38] and lightly revised in the 1983 *Code*.[39] Communion has been made available to those who have the use of reason and have completed seven years of age. In danger of death, children may receive Communion if they can distinguish the Body of Christ from ordinary food and receive it reverently.[40]

The first confession of sins had long been expected to precede the first reception of Communion, but no Church law ever explicitly demanded the practice. The 1917 *Code of Canon Law* required the confession of mortal sins,[41] and the 1983 *Code* required confession of serious sins once a year from

---

35 See *Quam singulari: Decree of the Sacred Congregation of the Discipline of the Sacraments on First Communion*, accessed September 1, 2014, http://www.papalencyclicals.net/Pius10/p10quam.htm.
36 See Craig, chap. 12, sect. 2.
37 See Craig, chap. 12, sect. 3.
38 See *Code of Canon Law*, 859 §1.
39 See *Code of Canon Law*, 11.
40 See *Code of Canon Law*, 913.
41 See *Code of Canon Law*, 901–902.

the age of discretion.⁴² The rules led some to question the necessity of First Confession before First Communion because of the unlikeliness that a child would commit mortal sin at such a young age. Consequently, some began to argue that the age of the use of reason for First Communion may precede the age of discretion for First Confession. The United States Conference of Catholic Bishops supported these ideas and recommended the deferral of First Confession until after First Communion in 1972. However, the Vatican declined to reverse the sequence in spite of the USCCB's appeal. Today the *Catechism of the Catholic Church* says that children "must go" to the Sacrament of Reconciliation before their First Communion.⁴³

There are various advantages to the traditional sequence. Although confession is not required for those without mortal sin, it does provide tremendous spiritual support for pursuing a faithful Christian life. All Catholics are entitled to the support that confession brings. By celebrating Reconciliation first, children learn at an early age the loving mercy of God, thus preparing them to appreciate more deeply the gift of Communion. They also gain a spiritual tool that will help them throughout their lives.

Fasting is another spiritual discipline that has long been associated with Communion. Practiced in some places as early as the fourth century, fasting had become a universal practice for anyone preparing to receive Communion. By the twentieth century, though, laws for fasting were becoming relaxed. In 1953 Pope Pius XII reaffirmed that Catholics should fast from midnight before coming to Communion. He made certain exceptions, though; for example, those who were sick could take some nourishment under certain conditions.⁴⁴ Four years later the same pope relaxed the rules much further, requiring only a three-hour fast before Communion.⁴⁵ In 1964 Pope Paul VI granted a further concession, reducing the fast to one hour before Communion.⁴⁶ That practice is still in force. It reminds the faithful to anticipate the holiness of the food and drink they receive at church. Fasting may express contrition for their sins or the joyful anticipation of Communion. Sometimes when people are very excited about an upcoming event, they naturally choose to fast.

---

42 See *Code of Canon Law*, 989.
43 See *Catechism of the Catholic Church*, 1457.
44 See *Christus Dominus*.
45 See *Sacram communionem: On Laws of Fasting and the Evening Mass*, accessed on September 1, 2004, http://www.papalencyclicals.net/Pius12/P12FAST.HTM.
46 See Paul VI, "Concession, on the eucharistic fast," announced at a public session of Vatican Council II, November 21, 1964: AAS 57 (1965), 186, DOL 272.

With the Second Vatican Council (1962–1965) the *Constitution on the Sacred Liturgy* called for a restoration of the catechumenate in stages, empowering priests to administer the Sacraments of Baptism, Confirmation, and Communion for previously unbaptized adults and children of catechetical age. For the first time in many centuries, First Communion was restored to the baptismal rite, and it was clearly once again a Sacrament of Initiation. Those baptized as infants continued to celebrate Confirmation and First Communion at a later date. Although the Second Vatican Council never clearly called these *deferred* events "Sacraments of Initiation," the *Catechism of the Catholic Church* did use that expression for the first time in any official Church document in 1992.[47] Now whenever Confirmation or First Communion are celebrated apart from Baptism, the Church considers them part of the Rites of Initiation.

Ever since the Middle Ages, the faithful received their Communion directly in the mouth. In 1969, the Vatican's Sacred Congregation for Divine Worship approved the option of receiving Communion in the hand in those Conferences of Bishops asking permission. This development happened because of renewed desire for sharing Communion at Mass, to recover some ancient liturgical practices, and to apply them where the signs and symbols fit today's culture. The American bishops made a formal request for the option of Communion in the hand, and the Vatican granted it in 1977. When the bishops implemented the permission, they explicitly extended it to children at their First Communion. "Careful preparation for first reception of the Eucharist will provide the necessary instruction"[48] for receiving Communion either on the tongue or in the hand. The choice is left to each of the communicants, even the very first time they receive.

Communion under both forms, another practice lost to the faithful from the Middle Ages, also came up for review. The Second Vatican Council's *Constitution on the Sacred Liturgy* permitted the faithful to receive Communion under both forms in certain circumstances. The 1967 instruction *Eucharisticum mysterium* says Communion has "a more perfect form when it is given under both species."[49] *The General Instruction of the Roman*

---

47 See *Catechism of the Catholic Church*, 1322.
48 "Appendix to the General Instruction for the Dioceses of the United States," *The Sacramentary* (New York: Catholic Book Publishing, 1985), pp. 51, 240.
49 Chupungco, p. 307.

Missal calls Communion under both forms a clearer sign of participating in the sacrifice actually being celebrated.[50]

To make the Eucharist even more available to communicants, concessions have been granted to those who are unable to consume normal bread or wine. In 2003 the Congregation for the Doctrine of the Faith established *Norms for Use of Low-Gluten Bread and Mustum*.[51] These do not allow gluten-free hosts, but do permit those that are low-gluten hosts. Mustum, a grape juice with suspended fermentation, is also valid for the Eucharist. These concessions apply not only to clergy, but to all the faithful, with permission of the bishop. Even children who may not be able to consume normal bread or wine may receive Communion under these alternative forms.

The Second Vatican Council's *Constitution on the Sacred Liturgy* repeatedly called for the full, conscious, active participation of the people at Mass, calling it even the aim to be considered before all others.[52] The Council introduced a shift in Catholic Eucharistic theology, one that can have a meaningful expression in the celebration of First Communion.

Prior to the Council, Catholics typically viewed the Mass as a celebration of the real presence of Christ under the form of the Eucharistic bread and wine. It differed from Benediction of the Blessed Sacrament primarily by the reception of Communion. Benediction had no Scripture readings as the Mass did, but Catholics were told that they could fulfill their obligation by coming to Mass as late as the offertory, having heard nothing from the Liturgy of the Word. As Benediction services were built on the premise that Christ should be adored in the consecrated bread, so the Mass paused for a few moments for the same purpose.

The highlight came during the Canon (now Eucharistic Prayer I), which the priest recited in Latin in a low voice, his back to the people. A bell signaled to the faithful that the consecration was imminent. They needed this assistance because the priest's progress in the canon was otherwise imperceptible. After repeating the words of Jesus concerning the bread, the priest genuflected and raised the consecrated host above his head for the adoration of the people. A server rang the bell. People looked briefly, then bowed their heads and whispered an acclamation such as, "My Lord and my God." The same happened moments later when the priest raised the chalice.

---

50 See *General Instruction of the Roman Missal*, 85.
51 See http://www.adoremus.org/CDF_Lowgluten-mustum2003.html, accessed September 1, 2014.
52 See *Constitution on the Sacred Liturgy*, 14.

This part of the service carried visual connections to Benediction, in which the priest raised the monstrance in order to bless the people. When people came for Communion at Mass, they experienced personal union with Christ, whose real presence they had adored earlier in the service.

The pre-Conciliar Communion Rite commonly kept a distance between the consecrated elements on the altar and the Communion of the faithful. People received Communion under one form, not two. The priest frequently distributed the people's Communion from the tabernacle, rather than from the altar. The tabernacle, the place of reposition of the uneaten consecrated hosts, had become the central focus of interior furnishings in a church. Because it housed the real presence of Christ, it naturally became the focus of adoration. People receiving Communion from the tabernacle made a connection once again between the host to be adored and the Communion to be received.

Although elements of these practices persist after the Second Vatican Council, the call for the full, conscious, active participation of the people pivoted the Eucharistic theology of the Mass. A paragraph from the *General Instruction of the Roman Missal*, already quoted above in part, shows the key difference in the view of what is happening at Mass:

> "It is most desirable that the faithful, just as the Priest himself is bound to do, receive the Lord's Body from hosts consecrated at the same Mass and that, in the cases where this is foreseen, they partake of the chalice (cf. no. 283), so that even by means of the signs Communion may stand out more clearly as a participation in the sacrifice actually being celebrated."[53]

The people are expected to participate in the sacrifice actually being celebrated. They are not present simply to adore or to receive Communion, but to participate in the sacrifice of Christ as well. At the Mass they become present to the sacrifice of Christ at Calvary; they enter into it in sacrament, and they join their own sacrifices to his, in hopes that their own will thus be acceptable to the Father. The faithful offer themselves together with the bread and wine.

As the bread and wine are transformed into the Body and Blood of Christ, the people are to share in the fruits of the sacrifice actually being celebrated by receiving Communion from the elements consecrated on the altar, not those reserved in the tabernacle. They are invited to receive under

---

[53] *General Instruction of the Roman Missal*, 85.

both forms—bread and wine—as a full sign of the sacrifice and covenant with God.[54]

Catholics have struggled to enliven this vision of the revised liturgy. Many of them still do not see the connection between the procession with the gifts and the procession to receive Communion. They are invited forward not simply to receive the fruit of their adoration, but the fruit of their offering.

Young children preparing for First Communion often miss this link as well. They know that they are missing out on Communion, but they may not realize that they are also missing out on offering. In order to share Communion with God fully, they should be fully sacrificing their lives to God as well.

Celebrations of First Communion often shine a spotlight on the child, as if he or she is the center of attention on this day. Relatives and friends shower gifts on the child, including medals, rosaries, statuettes, wall decorations, and books about the saints. Many of these support a personal piety that is peripheral to the Eucharist. They are not opposed to the Eucharist, but they invite children to think about the Mass as a time for each individual to adore Christ and to receive him in the heart.

Catholic Eucharistic theology demands something more. It demands the willingness to sacrifice. Part of First Communion preparation should invite children into acts of service, deeds of charity, and sacrifices for the sake of others and the Church. When they learn to give of their possessions for the sake

Good liturgical celebrations of First Communion will help prepare children for a lifetime of service.

of others, they are preparing to offer themselves to God with Christ. This is not just their First Communion with the real presence of Christ; it is their first participation in the sacrifice of the Mass with its demands for selfless

---

54 See Paul Turner, *My Sacrifice and Yours* (Chicago, IL: Liturgy Training Publications, 2014).

service. Full, conscious, active participation draws together a vibrant Christian life with the reception of Communion. Daily living in Christ prepares one for sacramental sharing in Christ, which in turn strengthens one to live in Christ each day of the week ahead.

Educators and clergy often express the fear that the First Communion will be the last time they see the child for some time to come. Many parents want their children to experience the ritual that other children have, but they are not prepared to make the weekly sacrifice it demands. Receiving Communion is always a blessed event, but it is far richer when coupled with a daily life of prayer and service, and when Sunday Mass becomes a regular habit.

The upcoming celebration of First Communion will be a memorable event for the child and the family. It will flow naturally out of a sweep of history that has found ways to blend many values of the faith. Celebrated well, it will prepare children for a lifetime of service and communion that will change them and the world forever.

Preparing the First Communion Liturgy

Anyone who has grown up in a Catholic household knows the celebration and reception of First Communion is a special time in the life of young children and their families. Most of us recall the day we first received Communion for the first time. It was a day filled with excitement and expectation, and that excitement continued Sunday after Sunday, as we were now able to join with our parents and older siblings in receiving Christ. Hopefully First Communion brings the same joy and excitement to Catholic families today.

It is a special time for children as they anxiously wait for the big day to arrive. They have been attending religious education classes or the parish school for a few years, where they have been learning about Jesus Christ and preparing for the day when they will receive Communion. It is a special time for parents, who see it not only as a rite of passage for their young children, but also as a time when their child engages in a deeper relationship with Christ and the Church. Parents also have been preparing by taking the children to Mass and to religious education classes. There may be special projects, activities, retreats, and prayer services that parents attend with or without the children. Then there is choosing the outfit that the child will wear for the special occasion. Many families host a party or dinner and invite others to share in their joy. The day becomes one that is fondly remembered for years to come.

First Communion is a special time for Catholic families and parishes.

It is also a special time in the life of the parish. With the reception of First Communion, a child is welcomed to be in communion with all those in the assembly of the faithful who are rightly disposed to receive the Sacrament of the Eucharist and thus belong more deeply to the Body of Christ.

The whole parish rejoices when children approach the Table of the Eucharist for the first time, for it shows the parish is alive and growing. The presence of the children brings smiles to the parishioners who have been praying for the children as they prepare for the big day.

The above is the ideal, but unfortunately sometimes First Communion loses some of its significance, especially among parents who, while wanting their children to receive First Communion, do not see all that goes along with it—such as adequate catechetical and spiritual preparation, Mass attendance, prayer, and a developing relationship with Christ—as being particularly important. For a significant number of parents, First Communion is more of a cultural event, something you have your child do simply because they are Catholic. Yet those of us who are responsible for preparing children to receive Eucharist, whether we be clergy, catechetical leaders, catechists and teachers, liturgists, musicians, and parents,[1] have a great responsibility to help children to come to love Christ and to understand that receiving First Communion is more than a day to dress up and have a party. It is a day that is one of the most important days of their young lives, a day when they become one with Christ when they receive his Body and Blood for the first time.

> All who have a part in the formation of children should consult and work together toward one objective: that even if children already have some feeling for God and the things of God, they may also experience in proportion to their age and personal development the human values that are present in the Eucharistic celebration.
>
> —*Directory for Masses with Children*, 9

Preparation Team

First Communion is a time of preparation and a joyous time for the parish community. For a year or more, catechists have been preparing young children to receive the Lord in the Eucharist for the first time. The religious education office has been busy assigning children to particular celebrations, printing worship aids, putting names on First Communion certificates, perhaps choosing gifts for the children, and making sure everything is well prepared. This can be daunting. It is important that all in the parish work

---

1 The *General Directory for Catechesis* teaches: "Parents are the primary educators in the faith. Together with them, especially in certain cultures, all members of the family play an active part in the education of the younger members" (255).

Preparing the First Communion Liturgy 23

The liturgies for First Communion should be prepared collaboratively.

together to make things go as smoothly as possible—and early on! It should not be the sole responsibility of the director of religious education (DRE) and his or her staff and catechists. It goes without saying that those responsible for preparing First Communion liturgies must be very familiar with the Church's liturgy. This point cannot be stressed enough. Communication and collaboration among the pastor, parochial vicars, deacons, the parish school, director of liturgy and music, and the liturgy committee are essential. Their collaborative work will ensure that the liturgies are meaningful and prepared appropriately. Since the celebration of the sacraments are never private, "but are celebrations belonging to the Church,"[2] the First Communion liturgy should never be prepared in isolation—there should always be good communication and collaboration among all those involved—from those teaching children, to those selecting music and preparing the environment, and to those who will preside over the liturgy.

Most often the preparation of the First Communion liturgy is left up to the DRE with input from the liturgy coordinator or music director. In some parishes, the DRE makes all the musical decisions for First Communion; in others, the director of liturgy and/or music chooses the music. This can lead to disagreements or hostility among the directors and staffs of these parish ministries, when each director has his or her ideas, and each believes that what he or she wants is right and best. Problems also occur when one or both directors have a poor understanding of the Church's liturgy. In an ideal situation, the DRE would have a good grasp of liturgical norms and be familiar with liturgical documents, especially those dealing with sacramental celebrations. In actuality, even though a person may be a good DRE, he or she may not have a background in the study of the Church's liturgy beyond the basics. The same holds true for some music directors. He or she may be an

---

2 *Constitution on the Sacred Liturgy*, 26.

excellent organist or choir director but lack the liturgical knowledge that is essential for providing appropriate music at certain liturgical celebrations. Lack of adequate knowledge of the liturgy is where problems begin.

Unfortunately a successful working relationship is not always present in a parish. There are many situations in which the DRE and liturgy or music director, the pastor and the DRE, the liturgy coordinator and pastor, and sometimes all of these, find themselves at odds with what should happen at pivotal sacramental celebrations. Sometimes a parish liturgy committee has input. When a parish school is involved, another group of people adds to the mix. Each comes armed with his or her ideas, with articles, with something heard at a workshop, or with various documents that make their point as to how the First Communion liturgy should be celebrated. Preparations for First Communion celebrations must begin with the parish's Sunday celebration of the Eucharist. It is in the Sunday liturgy where most of our parishioners encounter Christ. There should be ongoing evaluation by the parish staff and the liturgy committee, if there is one, concerning the liturgical practices in a parish.

There is no place in parish ministry for territorialism. As parish ministers, the DRE and liturgy or music director are all in service to the people of God in the parish. We do not own our particular ministry. The pastor, in order to provide a necessary service to the People of God, entrusts us as ministers to do what the Church calls us to do as servants. At times, we may have to put aside our ideas of how something should be done for the sake of the overall good of the parish and of the proper celebration of the Eucharistic liturgy.

It's always good practice to recognize our area of expertise and our limitations. When serving on the preparation team, those involved each do what they do best, and recognize the expertise that we have in our particular fields. Most of all, we know our limitations and when to ask others to assist us in areas where we lack the knowledge or experience.

We also need to ask the right questions. Just because someone wants to do something in the liturgy doesn't mean it is appropriate. When certain questions come up, we need to either know the answers or where to find them. For example, in some parishes, the children perform a song while standing in the sanctuary. This can be a major source of contention between the DRE and music director. The questions that must be asked are: Does this practice serve the assembly to grow closer to Christ? How does this draw us into the

Paschal Mystery? Who is it serving? Where does it draw our focus? Knowing where to find the answers and engaging in nonjudgmental discussions lead people on both sides to grow in their knowledge of liturgical norms.

We also need to know when to back down. There are times when, despite the fact that we are armed with all the right documents and reasoning why the music we believe is appropriate should be used at First Communion, we must recognize that the battle is best saved for another time. Perhaps the DRE, director of music and liturgy, school principal, or even the pastor insists on a particular hymn or choice of service music or psalm. This often happens when a piece of music becomes part of the "tradition" of the parish. If these issues have not been discussed early on, the month before First Communion is not the time to take a stand. The issue does not need to be dropped but perhaps put on the table for a year-end evaluation.

Above all, liturgical and catechetical ministers must be people of prayer. When disagreements occur, we need to bring the situation before the Lord and pray for the wisdom and knowledge that God's will be done, not ours. After all, we are doing the Lord's work.

First Communion as Evangelization

The celebration of First Communion often brings together family and friends who may not regularly participate in the liturgical life of the Church, may be alienated from the Church, or may not be Catholic or even Christian. This makes the celebration of First Communion an opportune moment of evangelization. Evangelization is "bringing the Good News into all the strata of humanity,"[3] where it will bring strength and renewal. Those who prepare the liturgy—every parish liturgy—share the responsibility of bringing Christ to others. Often we think of evangelization as bringing the Gospel to those who do not know Christ. But evangelization involves the deepening of one's relationship to Christ—our regular attendees as well as those who may have fallen away. Evangelization means we must help all Catholics

> Evangelization with joy becomes beauty in the liturgy, as part of our daily concern to spread goodness. The Church evangelizes and is herself evangelized through the beauty of the liturgy, which is both a celebration of the task of evangelization and the source of her renewed self-giving.
> —*Evangelii Gaudium*, 24

---
3 *Evangelii nuntiandi*, 18.

deepen their relationship with Christ and his Church. As the source and summit of our Christian lives,[4] the liturgy is the Church's primary means of evangelization. It is in the liturgy that we encounter Christ and receive him into our lives. Through participation in the liturgy, we are changed, fed, and nourished to be his disciples—his witnesses—in the world. The way we prepare the liturgy is essential for our mission of evangelization. Here are some key points for the parish preparation team to consider when preparing the First Communion liturgy:

Hospitality: It has been shown that the way people are treated when they come to church has a lot to do with their opinions and attitudes about the Church. The way we treat visitors and even long-time parishioners when they walk through our doors says much about who we are as a parish. If those in the assembly are one of the modes of the presence of Christ, then we need to truly consider how we greet people as they enter our churches. Hospitality ministers should be available at the door to greet visitors, to hand out worship aids, and to point out restrooms and the location of handicap and overflow seating. Visitors should be warmly welcomed and any questions cheerfully answered. We are happy that they are joining in our celebration. They should be available throughout the Mass to offer assistance, especially to those unfamiliar with Catholic worship or the worship of the particular parish. People who are made to feel welcome and comfortable will come away with a good feeling about the Church and about coming to Mass.

> The entire parish community, especially the parish leadership, must foster a spirit of hospitality and welcome. . . . [We must foster] a liturgical environment that invites, spiritually fulfills, and welcomes the full and active participation of the parish.
> —*Disciples Called to Witness*, p. 21

Good liturgy: Preparing the liturgy well is essential! Good liturgy is in itself an evangelizing moment. A liturgy done well has the ability to lift one's entire being to the Lord. So often parents remark that their child's First Communion celebration was the impetus for them returning to practicing the faith. Converts also have frequently remarked that it was an experience of the Mass, and especially the desire for the Eucharist, that brought them to faith. Allow the signs and symbols to be rich and meaningful. Schedule

---

[4] See *Constitution on the Sacred Liturgy*, 10; *Lumen gentium*, 11.

trained liturgical ministers. Be warm and welcoming to those in attendance.[5] Focus all liturgical preparations on the participation of the full assembly. At First Communion liturgies it can be a big temptation to include innovations and additions that take the focus off God, and liturgical participation, and focus primarily on the children. While it is an important day for the children, they are not the focus of our gathering; God is. When liturgies are prepared well, with God as our main focus, people notice. The liturgies will speak of beauty, reverence, peace, and a true sense of the presence of God. This sense of presence is part of evangelization. We want people to come face to face with God in the way we worship.

Well-prepared Music: Make sure the music is first rate. This means that instrumentalists and leaders of song should be the best the parish has to offer. Good music, just as good liturgy, has a way of strengthening faith. Liturgy and music done poorly has a way of turning people off to coming to Mass.[6] Not every parish can have a choir at First Communion liturgies, but they can make sure that those who are music ministers for these celebrations are well prepared and know how to lead others in sung prayer. Everyone may not join in the singing, although we hope they will, but music done well will touch their hearts in ways that words might not.[7]

Carefully written homilies: So often homilies at First Communion tend to gravitate toward the children even though there are many more adults present. For many people, the homily is the only place that they hear and learn about our faith. The homilist has an opportunity to reach people who may not be attending Mass regularly or at all. He has the opportunity to open their hearts to hearing the Word of God and entering into a relationship with the Divine. Speak to the children, yes, but also speak to the adults, and give them a message that will resonate in their hearts.[8]

Diocesan and Parish Guidelines

Before beginning to prepare the First Communion liturgies, parish staffs should consult guidelines prepared by their diocese. Sometimes the diocesan Office of Worship provides guidelines for the celebration of First Communion. Guidelines might also come from the office responsible for faith formation

---

5   See also pp. 40, 64, 67–68, 77, 110.
6   See *Sing To The Lord: Music in Divine Worship*, 5.
7   See pp. 41–45.
8   See p. 56.

and catechesis. For the most part, these guidelines focus mainly on the age at which children receive the sacrament, requirements for preparation for the sacrament, and what the children need to know before receiving. The guidelines discuss preparation of the parents as well and the importance of attending Sunday Mass each week. Some Offices of Worship, however, do provide detailed guidelines for those preparing the First Communion liturgies. Such guidelines are particularly helpful when First Communion will be celebrated at a separate Mass, although some dioceses request that First Communion only be celebrated at a parish Sunday Mass. Contact the diocesan Office of Worship for assistance in preparing the liturgy, or to answer questions. If such guidelines do not exist, it is important to convene with people responsible for preparing the liturgy, to develop parish guidelines, and to work together in preparing the liturgy. *Making Parish Policy: A Workbook on Sacramental Policies* by Ron Lewinski (published by Liturgy Training Publications) is a helpful resource for those establishing guidelines for any sacramental celebration in the parish. When establishing guidelines, be sure that they are grounded in liturgical norms. Always be cautious with suggestions found in catechetical journals or heard at catechetical workshops. While they may sound innovative and creative, often they vary from liturgical norms. Good educational practices do not usually make good liturgical practice. Upon hearing or reading something that is questionable, always check to see if it is conformity with the rites of the Church.

The Celebration of First Communion

Unlike the other sacramental rites, there is no "Rite of First Communion." A special ritual book is not used. It is a celebration of the Mass with those who are receiving Communion for the first time; therefore the rite that is followed and the prayer texts and readings that are used come from *The Roman Missal* and *The Lectionary for Mass*. When preparing the liturgy for First Communion, the same rubrics and liturgical principles used to celebrate the parish Sunday Mass should be followed.[9] The parish sacramental

---

9   Since there is no "ritual" for First Communion, parishes should also consult liturgical documents for preparing the Mass. The norms from the *General Instruction of the Roman Missal* (guidelines for the Mass), *Directory for Masses with Children* (guidelines for Masses with children), *Sing to the Lord: Music in Divine Worship* (guidelines for liturgical music), and *Built of Living Stones* (guidelines for liturgical environment) should be used. Important directives from these documents are included in this resource. Preparation teams might also consult the *Rite of Christian Initiation of Adults*, part II, section I. Although this part of the rite is for the full initiation of children who have

preparation team should decide upon the date for First Communion, determine what readings and prayers are used, and then reflect on these same readings and prayers to select music, determine environment needs, and decide upon other liturgical issues. When preparing these liturgies, the team must always "keep in mind that these eucharistic celebrations must lead children toward the celebration of Mass with adults, especially the Masses at which the Christian community must come together on Sundays,"[10] and bring the parish community—adults and children—together to celebrate the mystery of Christ's presence in the Eucharist fully, consciously, and actively.[11] The *Directory for Masses with Children* notes that when celebrating Masses with children in which a good number of adults are present, it is still "necessary to take great care that the children present do not feel neglected because of their inability to participate or to understand what happens and what is proclaimed in the celebration."[12] The celebration of First Communion is not all about the children. It is all about Christ and his giving us his Body and Blood in the Eucharist. It is about us as a community of believers participating in his sacrifice and receiving him. As a parish, we join with the children in celebrating what should be a long-awaited desire to receive Jesus and become one with him. Adults need to model this. "The witness of adult believers can have a great effect upon the children. Adults can in turn benefit spiritually from experiencing the part that the children have within the Christian community."[13] These are the principles that should guide First Communion preparation. The following section reviews the various liturgical needs and best practices to help parish teams in their preparation.

Scheduling First Communion

Liturgical Season

First Communion is often celebrated during Easter Time but it can be celebrated any time of the year. The *Code of Canon Law* does not specify a specific season for celebration. Celebrating during Easter Time maintains the reception of First Communion as a Sacrament of Initiation. Easter Time has a strong baptismal character and the parish most likely has initiated adults into the

---

reached catechetical age, the directives regarding the reception of Communion can be applied to First Communion liturgies.
  10 *Directory for Masses with Children*, 21.
  11 See *Constitution on the Sacred Liturgy*, 14.
  12 *Directory for Masses with Children*, 17.
  13 *Directory for Masses with Children*, 16.

faith at the Easter Vigil. Easter Time also falls at the end of the school year in which the children were prepared, which appears to make a lot of sense, but First Communion should not be seen as an end-of-the-school-year celebration.

First Communion may be celebrated other times of the year as well although it is probably best to avoid Advent and Lent. Celebrating at different times of the year may be a good way to proceed if the number of children receiving is large and First Communion is celebrated only at Sunday Mass. This might also work best if a parish does not have a resident priest and Communion services are usually celebrated. First Communion is only to be celebrated at Mass; therefore, scheduling a First Communion Mass during a liturgical season other than Easter Time may be necessary.

Sunday Mass

When scheduling First Communion liturgies, parish teams should decide if First Communion will be celebrated during parish Sunday Masses or at separate liturgies. Ideally, First Communion should be celebrated at a Sunday parish Mass with children receiving along with the community they and their families have been worshiping with all along. The celebration of the Sunday Eucharist is the most important aspect of the Christian life. Sunday Mass is the heart of the Christian week. It is the Lord's day, the day of Resurrection, the day of the Church—the day in which Christians gather to hear the Word and celebrate the Eucharist and to go forth, changed, as Christ's disciples.

> The Sunday celebration of the Lord's Day and his Eucharist is at the heart of the Church's life.
> —*Catechism of the Catholic Church*, 2177

Sunday is a day to celebrate community as the Body of Christ and our unity. From the double shares of Word and Sacrament we are nourished and then sent forth to live what we have celebrated. That living begins on Sunday itself.[14]

Pope John Paul II, in his document about the importance of Sunday, *Dies domini*, notes that "the Sunday eucharist expresses with greater emphasis its inherent ecclesial dimension. It becomes the paradigm for other eucharistic celebrations. Each community, gathering all its members for the

---

14 Joyce Anne Zimmerman, "An Overview of *Dies Domini: On Keeping the Lord's Day Holy*," found in *The Liturgy Documents: Volume I, Fifth Edition* (Chicago, IL: Liturgy Training Publications, 2012), p. 37.

'breaking of the bread,' becomes the place where the mystery of the church is concretely made present."[15] First Communion liturgies are a parish celebration and the assembly welcomes the children as they approach the Table of the Eucharist for the first time. The Sunday celebration, therefore, reinforces that children are now able to share in Communion, in union with the rest of the parish community. Receiving Communion for the first time is only the beginning of the fuller participation in the Christian community gathered together in prayer from Sunday to Sunday. The celebration of the sacraments are never private events, but part of the entire Body of Christ, the Church. As the *Rite of Christian Initiation of Adults* states, "initiation . . . is a gradual process that takes place *within the community of the faithful*."[16] What better liturgy is there for First Communion than the Sunday Mass?[17]

Practically, when deciding if a Sunday celebration is best for the parish, it must be determined how many children and their families can participate at each liturgy. There will be extra guests who need to be figured in the number, especially if pews are being reserved for the first communicants and their families. Parishes with large numbers of children preparing for First Communion might ascertain that it is impractical to have all the children receive at a single Sunday Mass; however, it can be worked out that children receive at multiple Sunday Masses on a particular day, different Sunday Masses over several weeks, or even at Sunday Masses throughout the year. It is important that the community is made aware of the presence of the first communicants, even announcing the week before that the children and their families will be attending particular Masses. While it should not create a problem, nor increase the length of the Mass, some parishioners appreciate the notice in order that there are no surprises when they discover they cannot sit in their favorite seat. If the parish is switching their policy to having First Communion at a Sunday Mass after the long practice of celebrating it on a Saturday, it is advisable to provide some catechesis for the parish, explaining the reason for the decision and why the parish Sunday liturgy is the preferred time and place

> Liturgical services are not private functions, but are celebrations belonging to the Church, which is the "sacrament of unity."
> — *Constitution on the Sacred Liturgy*, 26

---

15 *Dies domini*, 34.
16 *Rite of Christian Initiation of Adults*, 4 (emphasis added).
17 This also includes the Saturday evening Mass of anticipation for Sunday.

for First Communion. This can be mentioned in an article in the parish bulletin or in a letter sent home to parents. Priests and deacons may mention this in a liturgically-focused homily about the Eucharist and the Sunday Mass as the heart of the Christian week.

A parish must also set a policy on how families are chosen to attend a particular Mass if there are multiple Masses for First Communion. Some parishes determine this by class, with each class attending a different Mass. Some parishes offer parents a choice of which Mass they would like to attend. This can be accomplished on a first-come-first-serve basis to make it fair to all. Some parishes assign children by alphabetical order. Whichever way is chosen, be sure the parents have advance notice on how the Masses are assigned. In charity, allowances should be made for those who might have legitimate conflicts with the assigned dates.

Separate Masses

Although some dioceses do not recommend this practice, parishes may decide to have a separate First Communion Mass outside of the regularly scheduled parish Sunday Mass. This is something that many older parishioners might remember from their youth. Parishes with exceedingly large numbers of children receiving First Communion might find the practicality of this choice advantageous, since more children and their families and guests can be accommodated in the worship space. Many times these liturgies are celebrated on a Saturday morning or afternoon, or following the last scheduled Sunday Mass. More than one Mass may be scheduled on a single day, thus increasing the number of children receiving on a particular day. Assignment of the children to a particular Mass would be the same as if assigning them for a Sunday celebration of First Communion.

However practical the choice of a separate Mass may be, in a very real sense, it separates the children from the parish community. It also has the possibility of putting too much emphasis on the children instead of the reason why the children and the assembly are gathered—to celebrate the Eucharist with their parish community. Many times the children are put on display in various ways. Some parishes put additional focus on the children by using them as readers, having them stand in front of the assembly to sing a song, or by adding other elements to the liturgy. Just because this is not a regular Sunday Mass does not mean that good liturgical principles should be abandoned.

Catholic Schools and Parish Religious Education

When scheduling First Communion liturgies, parish staffs should be sensitive to children who participate in the parish religious education, are homeschooled, or attend a Catholic school. Some parishes schedule different Masses and assign the children and their families according to their schooling. "Participation in the faith life of the community is essential to an adequate understanding of the Eucharist. The practice of keeping separate First Communion celebrations of the parish school and religious education children . . . is working against an adequate understanding of parish community."[18] Parish preparation teams should ask the question, "When we separate the Catholic school children from the other children in our parish who are from public schools, private schools, or being homeschooled, what is that saying about the parish as a community?" A parish community comes together to celebrate significant moments. We welcome and treat all children the same. Segregating the two groups actually creates a "class" difference and sets them apart from the rest and unintentionally elevates one over the other. Although there may be practical reasons as to why a parish might want to keep the groups separate, upon deeper reflection, any reason disrupts the sense of community.[19]

If your parish practices this separation of Catholic school children and the children from other schools for First Communion, you might experience some resistance to changing this practice. It is important to be able to communicate the reasons for the decision and to assure parents that integrating the groups will not take away from the celebration but will enhance it.

Many of the children are probably well acquainted with each other from sports and other activities or from simply living on the same block. They may be involved in parish family activities together and attend the same Sunday Masses. If First Communion is celebrated at Sunday Mass, it is only natural for families who attend Mass together to celebrate this joyous occasion together. Catechists and teachers, DREs and principals, music ministers and liturgists, and clergy all need to work together to make it well prepared and beautiful for all the children and their families.

---

[18] Jo-Ann Metzdorff, "The Consumer Culture and Family Faith Formation, Practice and Preparation for First Holy Communion," (doctoral project, Seminary of the Immaculate Conception, 2007), p. 7.

[19] The same is true for celebrations of the Rite of Penance. When scheduling the Rite of Penance as a larger group, it is best to combine those from the parish religious education and those from Catholic schools. See also Appendix I.

If the decision is made to keep the celebrations separate, it is important to make sure that the liturgies are the same. Nothing creates more hard feelings than to have something done at the Catholic school First Communion liturgy that is not done at the other liturgies for the children in the parish religious education program. The worship aids, music, readings, and prayers should all be the same—changing these elements because of the day of the celebration. Providing other opportunities to come together before or after the First Communion Masses also helps to integrate both groups.

Another concern is with regard to children who attend a particular parish school but live in a different parish. Many dioceses require that children receive their sacraments in the parish at which the family resides, not the parish where they attend Catholic school. This brings up the question as to where they are to prepare for First Communion, in the school they attend or at their parish. Much depends upon how the parish prepares the children.

Seating

The parish preparation team will need to discuss the children's seating arrangements. There are different arrangements for seating children and their families for First Communion Masses. Often times, the model a parish chooses depends on how many children are receiving at a particular Mass. Parish preparation teams would do well to evaluate existing parish practice each year. The following models might be considered.

There was a time, not too long ago, when all first communicants sat together, boys on one side, girls on the other side of the center aisle, in size order and in straight rows one head behind the other with space in between. These were separate First Communion Masses, usually on a Saturday. In the 1970s and '80s many parishes moved to celebrating First Communion at a Sunday parish liturgy. In a desire to emphasize the importance of the family worshipping together, they began to have the children sitting with their parents and family as they would on any other Sunday instead of the children by themselves as a group. This type of arrangement better signifies the communal aspect of receiving Communion and the fact that it is not "all about the first communicants" but about their sharing in the Eucharist.

There are a few possibilities for this model. Each family would be seated in a reserved pew and the children would be seated on the ends, often with a banner with the child's name on it, but this is not necessary. This arrangement also became common at separate First Communion liturgies in order to emphasize the importance of the family in both the preparation of the children for First Communion and in celebrating the sacrament as a family. Many parishes continue to use this seating arrangement today. If one row is not enough for the entire family—including extended family and guests—extra rows can be reserved, or additional guests can be asked to sit elsewhere, behind the last of the reserved rows.

In another model, children can be seated only with their parents in those pews closest to the sanctuary. Family and friends are seated elsewhere. An advantage to this model is that there are fewer distractions from family members and all the first communicants are seated in the same area

Children may be seated with their parents in those pews closest to the sanctuary.

of the church. This works well with a large number of children who otherwise would have been spread throughout the church if each family had their own row. Using this model, children can process in by themselves before the entrance procession begins or as part of the entrance procession. There is also the option of not having the children as part of the entrance procession but already seated with their parents before the liturgy begins. A disadvantage to this is separating the children from the entire family and losing a bit of the communal aspect of the assembly.

An option that is not particularly common is to have the children seated with their families as they would on any Sunday. The families would be spread out among the rest of the assembly, sitting wherever they desire and not in reserved seating. This option takes much of the focus off the children, but emphasizes their importance as members of the assembly. This might work well in a smaller parish where most of the families already participate in Sunday Eucharist and where the children, parents, and parishioners have been well catechized on the role of the assembly. The children would not be included in the procession unless it is well planned that the children will be sitting at the ends of the pews, but since it won't be determined ahead of time where they will sit, it is better not to have them process in. This also takes the emphasis off the children as it truly makes them part of the assembly.

There are a few concerns with regard to this model. The first concern would be having enough seating together for the entire family and any guests. If the Mass is crowded and the family or guest arrive late, they may not all be able to be seated together. This can be solved by asking the families to arrive at least fifteen minutes early so they can find seats together. Otherwise extended family and guests would just sit wherever they find seating. Another concern occurs when it comes time to receive Communion. In this model, the children would simply take their place in the Communion procession with all those who are receiving. Since children are expected to receive their First Communion, or at least the host, from a priest, if there are a number of Communion ministers it will be necessary to make sure the children approach the priest first to receive the host, before receiving from the cup, held by an extraordinary minister of Holy Communion. It can be confusing, but a well-placed usher can direct the children to the priest as they approach the front of the Communion line, provided the children are wearing identifiable attire. Children and parents can be reminded that they must go to the priest, but amid the excitement of the moment, both children and parents can forget. If the children are not dressed in First Communion attire it might make identifying them more difficult. The first communicants can also be called up first, but again this would defeat the purpose of having them receive as part of the assembly and not standing apart from them.

Some parishes also have children sitting together; sometimes boys on one side, girls on the other side, or mixed. Pastoral teams who have chosen this model contend that this arrangement prevents some of the problems they have observed when families sit in the same pew with the first communicants. They offer the observation that the children are less focused and often distracted by siblings and family members when sitting with them. Other pastoral leaders notice that with the growing number of divorced and separated parents, conflicts unfortunately arise when it comes to seating at sacramental celebrations. In an ideal world, divorced or separated parents put aside any animosity for the sake of their children, but often these celebrations exacerbate the situation, putting the children in the middle. Seating all the children together avoids this situation as parents can sit where they prefer to sit instead of in reserved rows.

Parents will need to be informed ahead of time where their children will be seated. It might be helpful to provide a seating chart noting where families will be seated. Communicate any changes ahead of time, and provide adequate explanations for the changes. Expect that some parents will express disappointment or even some anger if changes are being made to long-standing parish traditions for sacramental celebrations. Be open to hearing their concerns and always assure them that the celebration will be beautiful and that the focus is always on receiving Christ, not on the externals. On the day of the celebration, pews might need to be reserved to avoid confusion.

There are parishes that celebrate First Communion many times during the year with small groups of only one or two or just a few children spread out over many Sundays. A parish might be so small, or it may be a mission church, that only has a small number of children receiving. In these cases, sometimes parents, in consultation with the pastor or DRE, decide which particular Sunday they want their child to receive. It is best though to avoid Advent and Lent as you don't want to take away from the particular focus of these seasons. The children and their family can be seated in reserved rows in the front, or throughout the assembly. They can process in or simply be seated with their family. They should be recognized in some way by the presider and perhaps receive Communion first with their family before the rest of the assembly. It happens at times that a child is ill when their class or group receives First Communion. In such a case, this model is appropriate for them as well. There may be a situation where a child is hospitalized. If it is not a serious condition, the family can wait until the child recovers and then receive their First Communion at a parish Sunday Mass. For serious conditions, a priest can always bring the Eucharist to a child and they can receive with family present in the hospital without it being a Mass. The rites for Communion to the Sick would be used.

Liturgical Ministers

When preparing a First Communion liturgy, the children's role in the liturgy is always a question. Some parishes may have children serve as readers, gift bearers, or song leader. Others find something for every child to do in order that no one feels excluded. It is important to keep in mind that being part of the assembly is a very important role and essential to the integrity of the liturgy. "In the celebration of the Mass the faithful form a holy people, a people of God's own possession and a royal Priesthood, so that they may give thanks to God"[20] and unite their sacrifice with Christ's sacrifice.

Some might argue, citing the *Directory for Masses with Children*, that children should be involved in liturgical ministries according to their abilities.[21] After all, this is their First Communion Mass and we want them to be engaged! There is no denying that it is a good thing to involve children at Mass, and there are many ways children can participate, but the question that must be asked is if their First Communion liturgy is the best place for them to serve a role in the liturgy. This is the first time they will receive Communion and will be welcomed at the Eucharistic table. At this special Mass they should be ministered to instead of ministering to others. This is a time when the children need to focus simply on preparing to receive the Lord, and participating to the best of their ability in the Mass. That is their role at the First Communion liturgy. Whenever you come to worship, even if you are not serving as a liturgical minister, you serve as a minister of the assembly, as one who prays and sings. "Christ is really present in the very assembly gathered in his name."[22] He is present when the Church, the gathered assembly, prays and sings. Each of us has a part to play at Mass. Together we form the Body of Christ. Our participation in the liturgy is our important role. There are other opportunities to engage children in ministries during both their time of preparation at grade level or class liturgies, prayer services, or devotional activities.

While there is nothing prohibiting them from serving in the liturgical roles, it is good to prayerfully reflect on what assigning children roles could signify. If the First Communion group is large, there will be only a few who get assigned roles. How are they chosen? Are the class favorites or children of the catechists asked, leaving others out? Are the children chosen at random, or on merit? You have to consider that there will be hurt feelings among some of the children not chosen, not to mention parents who feel that their child should be doing something at Mass. Not choosing children for roles in

---

20 *General Instruction of the Roman Missal*, 95.
21 See *Directory for Masses with Children*, 22. Please note that this directive is also found under the heading, "Masses with Children in which only a few adults participate." This implies school Masses. Under the heading "Masses with adults in which children also participate," the *Directory for Masses with Children* notes "it may also be helpful to give some task to the children. They may, for example, bring forward the gifts or perform one of the other songs of the Mass" (18). First Communion would be a Mass in which adults are present. Although this directive encourages children to participate in liturgical roles, this does not meant the first communicants take on this role. Other trained children can participate.
22 *General Instruction of the Roman Missal*, 27.

the First Communion liturgy eliminates all these concerns. There will always be other opportunities for children to serve as they get older and more involved in parish life.

There are certain functions which those who have been trained and properly formed fulfill. Children, and especially parents, need to be aware that not having a "job" during the liturgy does not make the child's participation any less "special." Liturgical ministries should be filled by trained parishioners.[23] The child's very important role is to participate in the Mass and be brought into full Communion at the Eucharistic table.

There are probably a number of parents or other relatives among the First Communion families that are involved in liturgical ministry in the parish. You can call upon these people to serve as hospitality ministers, readers, extraordinary ministers of Holy Communion, psalmist, or leader of song. If there is an older sibling of a first communicant who is an altar server, they can be asked to serve at the liturgy. Siblings or members of last year's First Communion class can be asked to assist the ministers of hospitality, helping to seat people and hand out worship aids. Take into consideration, however, that families might prefer to be together with their first communicant at this time. They might prefer to be ministered to rather than to be involved in ministry at this liturgy. Those teens or younger children who are also parish readers, cantors, or leaders of song can serve in that capacity at the First Communion Mass.[24]

If they have been trained, teens and younger children may serve as liturgical ministers.

---

23 This is not to say that children should not serve as liturgical ministers; however, at this liturgy, the children receiving First Communion are being ministered to. It's best to consider them as liturgical ministers at other liturgies.

24 Because there will most likely be many guests attending the liturgy, great care should be given to those who serve as cantor, psalmist, or leader of song. A liturgy of this nature will require a skilled minister; one who not only has strong musical skills but is confident in their gesture and in leading.

Consider inviting the children's choir and youth choir to lend their voices and instruments to the main choir.

Don't overlook the catechists or the parish school teachers who might be trained liturgical ministers. They would be most happy to assist in the different ministries at the First Communion Mass when their students receive First Communion. Those who are not liturgical ministers can also assist in helping gather the children before Mass, line up for the procession, seat them, and assist during the liturgy.

If family members who are liturgical ministers prefer to remain in the pews with their children, regular parish liturgical ministers can be scheduled to serve at First Communion Masses, especially if First Communion is celebrated at a Sunday Mass. When First Communion is celebrated as a parish event, then the participation of those in the parish shows this clearly. In this case, the ministers used should be the ones regularly scheduled for the particular liturgy, although special requests from parish liturgical ministers who are related to or friends of first communicants should be honored. Those asked to serve need to be made aware of anything out of the ordinary that they may be asked to do.

Selecting Music

Sing to the Lord: Music in Divine Worship provides the criteria for judging the suitability of music for the liturgy. There are three judgments: the liturgical, the pastoral, and the musical.

Liturgical: The first criterion is liturgical. The music must be appropriate for the particular liturgical celebration. The following must be asked: "Is this composition capable of meeting the structural and textual requirements set forth by the liturgical books for this particular rite?"[25] Are the pieces chosen appropriate for Mass or are they basically songs that are catechetical and better restricted to the classroom? This is one of the areas of disagreement that could occur between the DRE and music director. There are many songs that are suggested or recommended to be part of a religious education program. Here is where good communication between the DRE and the music director is important. If there is a musical component that accompanies the parish's religious education text series, it is beneficial for the DRE to provide the music director with a copy of the music or the CD. Sometimes the

---

25 *Sing to the Lord: Music in Divine Worship*, 127.

Preparing the First Communion Liturgy

religious education program includes a theme song. If this song is appropriate for liturgy, it can be used at Sunday Mass or other liturgies involving both the school (if there is one) and religious education children and sung by a children's choir (if there is one). However, not all of the songs in our programs are appropriate for the liturgy. They do not fit the criterion of being liturgical. Musical selections should fit the specific liturgical action at the part of the Mass when they will be used. The entrance song should evoke a sense of gathering the assembly to prepare to celebrate the liturgy. During the procession to receive Communion, the texts should support the action of receiving the Eucharist. "A certain balance among the various elements of the Liturgy should be sought, so that less important elements do not overshadow more important ones. Textual elements include the ability of a musical setting to support the liturgical text and to convey meaning faithful to the teaching of the Church."[26]

> Singing is one of the primary ways that the assembly of the faithful participates actively in the Liturgy. . . . So that the holy people may sing with one voice, the music must be within its members' capability.
>
> —*Sing to the Lord: Music in Divine Worship,* 26 and 27

Pastoral: The second criterion is the pastoral judgment. "The pastoral judgment takes into consideration the actual community gathered to celebrate in a particular place at a particular time. Does a musical composition promote the sanctification of the members of the liturgical assembly by drawing them closer to the holy mysteries being celebrated? Does it strengthen their formation in faith by opening their hearts to the mystery being celebrated on this occasion or in this season? Is it capable of expressing the faith that God has planted in their hearts and summoned them to celebrate?"[27] This judgment is probably the most important to consider when preparing First Communion liturgies, because included in this judgment is the ability of the children to sing and understand the songs. It is in this area where some conflicts might arise. *Sing to the Lord* states, "One should never underestimate the ability of persons of all ages, cultures, languages, and levels of education to learn something new and to understand things that are properly and thoroughly introduced."[28] Music directors, especially those who direct children's choirs, know that children, even at a young age, can sing and under-

---

26 *Sing to the Lord: Music in Divine Worship*, 128.
27 *Sing to the Lord: Music in Divine Worship*, 130.
28 *Sing to the Lord: Music in Divine Worship*, 132.

stand pieces that others might think are beyond the capability of this age group. The key is in the introduction of the music to the children. Since music has the ability to open people's hearts to Christ, the music selected for First Communion should also be considered among the catechetical resources utilized in the religious education program. The assistance of the director of music is imperative here. Also, if the parish is bilingual or includes different cultures, that should be considered with regard to the choice of music.

Musical: The final criterion is musical. The music must be good, well prepared, and performed well. "Is this composition technically, aesthetically, and expressively worthy?"[29] This judgment is basic and primary and should be made by competent musicians. Only artistically sound music will be effective in the long run. "To admit to the Liturgy the cheap, the trite, or the musical cliché often found in secular popular songs is to cheapen the liturgy, to expose it to ridicule, and to invite failure."[30] Many times a DRE or an inexperienced music director might assume that since the celebration involves children, the music should be geared toward children. They choose music that is childish or cliché. Music lines may be excessively simple or basic and the texts lacking any real theology. When good liturgical music is chosen and taught to the children, we are aiding them in developing a love of liturgical music, and good music in general, that it is hoped will remain part of them for the rest of their lives. We do children a disservice to limit their repertoire to music that is trite or part of the latest fad. Good music, whether it is traditional or contemporary, stands the test of time. When choosing music, however, we must consider the ability of the assembly to participate in singing. It is important to choose music that the assembly will be familiar with, and refrains that are easy to follow. Introducing new music at a celebration of First Communion will guarantee that the assembly will not sing. What kind of accompaniment will there be? The DRE might be partial to piano or guitars, but is that what the parish community is used to hearing on Sunday? Is the parish repertoire traditional or contemporary, or is it a mix of both? These are important questions that must be considered when deciding on music for all parish celebrations, and especially sacramental celebrations.

> "All three judgments must be considered together, and no individual judgment can be applied in isolation from the other two. This evaluation requires cooperation, consultation, collaboration, and mutual respect

---

29 *Sing to the Lord: Music in Divine Worship*, 134.
30 *Sing to the Lord: Music in Divine Worship*, 135.

among those who are skilled in any of the three judgments, be they pastors, musicians, liturgists, or planners."[31]

"The choice of individual compositions for congregational participation will often depend on those ways in which a particular group finds it best to join their hearts and minds to the liturgical action."[32] Music is such an important part of any liturgical celebration and First Communion liturgies are no exception. "Singing must be given great importance in all celebrations, but it is to be especially encouraged in every way for Masses celebrated with children, in view of their special affinity for music."[33] We need to encourage singing at our First Communion liturgies, and children love to sing, but we must be careful not to make it into a performance. We need to keep in the forefront the reason why we are gathering. We also must be aware that, for the most part, the majority of the assembly will be adults. "The role of music is to serve the needs of the Liturgy and not to dominate it, seek to entertain, or draw attention to itself or the musicians. . . . The primary role of music in the Liturgy is to help the members of the gathered assembly to join themselves with the action of Christ and to give voice to the gift of faith."[34]

Music should always be prepared in consultation with the parish liturgy and music director.[35] The community's repertoire should be considered when selecting music for First Communion—this includes the selection of hymns and songs as well as the settings for the acclamations and responses. Selecting songs and acclamations that are used for the regular parish Masses will help the assembly participate more fully at First Communion liturgies regardless if it is a separate liturgy or during Sunday Mass. "Great importance should therefore be attached to the use of singing in the celebration of the Mass, with due consideration for the culture of peoples and abilities of each liturgical assembly."[36]

Occasionally a new song or hymn might be introduced for First Communion. It's best not to introduce this song the day of the celebration. Prepare to incorporate the song into the parish liturgies leading up to First Communion. Use it in the classroom or in prayer services. This is also not the time to introduce new acclamations or Mass settings. Use the setting that

---

31 See *Sing to the Lord: Music in Divine Worship*, 126.
32 *Sing to the Lord: Music in Divine Worship*, 70.
33 *Directory for Masses with Children*, 30.
34 *Sing to the Lord: Music in Divine Worship*, 125.
35 See p. 23 regarding the importance of collaborating with the parish staff.
36 *General Instruction of the Roman Missal*, 40.

has been used at Sunday Mass. For example, if First Communion is scheduled during Easter Time, use the setting that the parish uses during that season.

If a choir usually sings at the Sunday Mass in which First Communion is scheduled, by all means continue to use the choir to help sustain the singing, but perhaps choose music that is more manageable for young singers to join in singing.

In order for children to participate at Mass with the songs and acclamations, it is a good idea to rehearse with them the music that has been prepared for the First Communion liturgy. This can be done during their religious education class. Invite the parish music director or another capable musician to lead this rehearsal with the children either in the classroom or in the church. If your parish has a children's choir and some of the choir members are also receiving First Communion, they will probably enjoy helping the other children learn the songs and acclamations.

On the day of First Communion, it might be necessary to rehearse some of the music with the assembly before the liturgy begins. Some parishes already rehearse music routinely before Mass begins and it is necessary if there are a good number of guests who are not from the parish, especially if the celebration of First Communion is at a separate liturgy rather than the parish Sunday Mass.

Liturgical Environment

Preparing the environment in the church for First Communion should follow the same principles used for any other parish liturgy. It's not necessary to adorn the church with excessive flowers, banners, pew decorations, and other adornments. Those who prepare the liturgy should ask, "do the decorations enhance or detract from the principal action of the Mass—the reception of First Communion?" When preparing the environment for First Communion, the parish environment team should be consulted. Be sure to "include other areas beside the sanctuary," ensuring that "the altar should remain clear and free-standing,"[37] and other liturgical actions should not be blocked. Be attentive to the altar, the ambo, where the assembly gathers, and the presidential chair.

Flowers: When using flowers, living plants and flowers should always be used, and additional arrangements besides what are used for the regular Sunday Mass are not necessary. Consider arrangements indigenous to your

---

37 *Built of Living Stones*, 124.

local area or region. If celebrating during Easter Time replace any of the flowers which may have died or wilted. Try to keep or replace some of the Easter flowers to again make that connection with the Easter sacraments.[38]

Banners and Hangings: It is the tradition in some parishes to have the children and their parents make a banner that will be placed on the end of the pew where the child and family will be seated. The banners usually consist of Eucharistic symbols and the name of the child so that they can easily find their seat. While these banners are a nice touch, caution should be taken that the banners do not become a point of distraction or create a sense of competition. The use of white bows or other simple decoration on the ends of the pews is another way to mark off those pews being utilized by the first communicants, especially if parents and family will not be seated with the children. The use of a processional banner or other banners placed in specific locations throughout the church add to the festivity of the celebration yet, as with other seasonal decorations, they should not draw attention away from but lead to the celebration of the Eucharist. Of course, reserved signs can also be used in lieu of banners and bows. Additional banners can be made for the entrance procession and fabric hangings to adorn the gathering space or narthex and inside of the church. "Fabric art . . . can be an effective way to convey the spirit [of the liturgy] . . . through the use of color, shape, texture, and symbolic form. The use of images rather than words is more in keeping with this medium."[39]

> Decorations are intended to draw people to the true nature of the mystery being celebrated rather than being ends in themselves. Natural flowers, plants, wreaths and fabric hangings, and other seasonal objects can be arranged to enhance the primary liturgical points of focus. The altar should remain clear and free-standing, not walled in by massive floral displays, . . . and pathways in the narthex, nave, and sanctuary should remain clear.
>
> —*Built of Living Stones,* 124

Vessels, Vestments, and Altar Cloths: Use the best that the parish has, those that you might use for great solemnities and feasts such as Christmas and Easter.

Colors: When First Communion is celebrated the color of the particular Mass is used. If First Communion takes place at Sunday Masses

---

38 See *Built of Living Stones,* 129.
39 *Built of Living Stones,* 127.

throughout the year, the color of the Sunday is used. For First Communion Masses that are scheduled separately, white is usually used. Hints of gold and silver could be used as well.

Other decorations: As with all decorations, they should not distract from the celebration, but enhance it and add to the dignity of the celebration. Candles are used at every celebration of the Mass. Instead of two candles you might want to consider using four or six.[40] Unconventional decorations that have little to do with liturgy or the sacrament of the Eucharist are to be avoided. The environment should enhance the liturgical rites not distract. Noble simplicity is a norm that should be observed at all liturgies, including and notwithstanding sacramental celebrations.

Reverence in Church

Whenever a large number of people come to church for sacramental celebrations, there usually is an exceptional amount of talking before the Mass begins—much more than we would experience at a regular parish Mass. Part of the reason is the excitement on the part of the families and guests, but many times the reason is because of many people who do not usually attend Mass or who are not Catholic and are unaware of the attitude of reverence that most of us are used to. Hopefully parents and their children have been attending Mass weekly, especially since they are preparing for First Communion, but even if this is so, it seems that this Mass is out of the ordinary and families greeting each other and getting ready for the Mass to begin. It is certainly understandable since this is a very happy occasion. Yet if First Communion is being celebrated at a regular parish Sunday Mass where the assembly is used to a quiet time of preparation before the liturgy begins, you don't want to generate negative feelings among the regulars in the assembly. While some talking above what is normally experienced may be expected to occur, you do want to maintain a sense of reverence being in the presence of the sacred.

> The rites should be marked by a noble simplicity; they should be short, clear, and unencumbered by useless repetitions; they should be within the people's powers of comprehension and as a rule not require much explanation.
> —*Constitution on the Sacred Liturgy*, 34

---

40 See *General Instruction of the Roman Missal*, 117.

It might be beneficial to make an announcement about ten minutes before the liturgy begins, gently reminding those attending that they are in the presence of the Blessed Sacrament (or in a sacred space if the tabernacle is in a separate chapel) and request that they use this time to pray for the children who will be receiving First Communion. Hopefully this will solve the problem and the announcement will not have to be made again. Keeping the request positive will have a greater effect on those in the assembly, rather than just asking them to be quiet. Announcements may not be necessary if the music ministry provides instrumental or choral preludes as people gather. They will quiet down so as to enjoy the music. Rehearsing songs and/or acclamations can also be done at this time, which will reduce the chatter. Keeping the amount of preparation activity in the church to a minimum before the liturgy begins will help people to focus on prayer, as people moving around setting things up tends to be disruptive and indirectly suggests that the people can be casual until the celebration begins.

The First Communion Liturgy

The Order of Mass

As noted above, there is no "Rite of First Communion." The liturgy for First Communion follows the Order of Mass as found in *The Roman Missal*. The prayers that are used from the Missal are determined by the date when First Communion is celebrated—the Collect, Prayer over the Offerings, Preface, and Prayer after Communion. For example, if First Communion is scheduled during the Sunday Masses on the Fourth Sunday of Easter, the prayers must be from that Sunday as found in the Missal. There is more flexibility with the selection of prayer texts if First Communion is celebrated on a weekday[41] or a Sunday afternoon.[42] Ritual Masses, like First Communion, may be scheduled on these days and the prayers that are used do not have to come from the Mass of the day (although, this is certainly an option). If, for example, First Communion is scheduled on Saturday morning and the Mass of the day is a memorial of a saint, the prayers do not need to come from the saint's day. Instead, *The Roman Missal* includes special texts for Votive Masses (Mass for a special intention), among them a Votive Mass for the Most Holy Eucharist

---

41 Except for those during the Octave of Easter, or on a solemnity, the Commemoration of All the Faithful Departed, Ash Wednesday, or on the weekdays of Holy Week.

42 Except if Sunday occurs during the seasons of Advent, Lent, and Easter, on a solemnity, or on the Commemoration of All the Faithful Departed.

(found at #5 in the Votive Mass section of *The Roman Missal*). If this Mass is celebrated, the color is white (even during Advent or Lent),[43] and the Preface of the Most Holy Eucharist is used. *The Roman Missal* also provides this option, "As a Votive Mass of the Most Holy Eucharist, the Votive Mass of our Lord Jesus Christ, the Eternal High Priest may also be used, . . . or the Mass of the Solemnity of the Most Holy Body and Blood of Christ." The Preface of the Most Holy Eucharist is still used with Mass for Jesus Christ, the Eternal High Priest. If the text for the Solemnity of the Most Holy Body and Blood are used, the Preface is proper. Please note that the Missal provides chanted text for the Prefaces. The parish music director should consult with the priest celebrant about using this option.

Consider using incense at the appropriate places—to incense the cross and the altar after the opening procession; during the procession with the *Book of the Gospels*; to incense the gifts after they are placed on the altar, along with the cross the altar itself, and the priest, deacon, and assembly before the Prayer over the Offerings; and during the elevation at the Consecration. Also be attentive to where silence is called for—after "Let us pray," following the invitation to pray in the Penitential Act, after the readings and the homily, and after the reception of Communion.

The Gloria should be sung or said (except during Advent and Lent). If First Communion takes place during a Sunday Mass, the Creed should be sung or said.

Any of the four Eucharistic Prayers may be used. It is not recommended that priest celebrants use the Eucharistic Prayers for Masses with Children. Included in the previous Sacramentary, these prayers were adapted for the cognitive needs of children and include additional acclamations. When the third edition of *The Roman Missal* was prepared and promulgated, these prayers were removed from the Missal because they did not appear in the original Latin text. However, the United States Conference of Catholic Bishops received permission to update these texts and publish them as a supplement to the Missal. An introductory document regarding the use of these prayers is included in the supplement and states that "the use of these prayers is strictly limited to Masses celebrated with children. The right of the Bishop,

---

43 If First Communion is celebrated on a Sunday, the color is determined by the Sunday. For example, if First Communion takes place on a Sunday during Easter Time, the color is white. If First Communion takes place on a Sunday in Ordinary Time, the color is usually green (unless the Sunday of Ordinary Time is a solemnity, such as the Solemnity of the Most Holy Body and Blood of Christ, in which case, the color is white).

which is determined in the *Directory for Masses with Children*, remains, however, intact."[44] The *Directory for Masses with Children* states, "If the number of children is large, it may at times be suitable to plan the Mass so that it corresponds more closely to the needs of the children."[45] The directive is clear that adaptations are to be made when it is a large number of children. Even though a First Communion liturgy involves a child's first reception of Communion, there will still be a large number of adults present, especially if First Communion occurs during Sunday Mass. It is best to avoid the Eucharistic Prayers for Masses with Children at a parish First Communion liturgy. These prayers are best used for school liturgies.

The Introductory Rites

The Introductory Rites open the celebration and help the assembled people to "come together as one,"[46] preparing them to hear God's Word and to celebrate the Eucharist. At First Communion liturgies, the Introductory Rites include the entrance song and procession, Sign of the Cross and Greeting, Penitential Act and Kyrie or Rite of Sprinkling, Gloria, and the Collect. Although it is a regular liturgy with no "special rites" during this part of the Mass, the following should be considered.

Entrance Procession

The entrance procession helps the assembly to focus on our gathering as a community of the faithful to celebrate the liturgy. It also symbolizes that we are all on a journey, a journey of faith. The cross leads the ministers through midst of the assembly. The usual order for the procession is a thurifer (if incense is used), server with the cross, servers with candles (standing on either side of the cross), the deacon, and the priest celebrant. If concelebrants are present they follow the deacon and precede the priest celebrant. The deacon carries the *Book of the Gospels* or, if there is no deacon, a reader performs this function. Even though the entrance procession is for the ministers of the liturgy, many parishes, following a long tradition, have the children incorporated into the entrance procession. This needs to be discussed with the committee preparing the liturgy and diocesan guidelines, if there are any, should be consulted.

---

44 *Eucharistic Prayers for Masses with Children: Introduction*, 14.
45 *Directory for Masses with Children*, 19.
46 *General Instruction of the Roman Missal*, 46.

The children may be seated before the liturgy begins and not take part in the procession. Since the entrance procession is for those ministering during the Mass, there is no obligation to have the children participate, as they are not ministers. In a very real way, they are the ones being ministered to on this special occasion of their First Communion. It is best to ask the families to arrive and get settled in their places at least fifteen minutes before Mass is scheduled to begin. This will help to avoid any latecomers running down the aisle after the liturgy starts.

Parishes often have the children process into the worship space before the actual beginning of the liturgy, and be in their places before the entrance song begins. They can double up or process single file. The children precede the processional cross. A banner-bearer can lead the children in procession while instrumental music is played. Once the children are at their seats, the entrance or gathering song can begin. This option enables the children to participate in the singing of the entrance or gathering song instead of trying to have them sing as they are processing. If the children are singing while they are processing they can become easily distracted by the excitement and nervousness of the moment.

Children can also be included in the entrance procession. The cross-bearer and servers with candles lead the procession. A banner-bearer may follow the servers and lead the children into the worship space. Another banner-bearer can precede the remaining liturgical ministers, deacon, and priest celebrant. If a banner-bearer is not included here, the deacon and priest celebrant follow the children.

If children are included in a procession, either before or during the entrance procession, catechists will need to instruct them to reverence the altar. Once the children have processed down the main aisle, they are to reverence the altar with a profound bow (bow at the waist). It is a beautiful sight and a great example to the rest of the assembly to see the children do this simple but profound act. As with many aspects of the First Communion liturgy, this needs to be rehearsed well. Upon entering their pew, remind the children to remain standing to sing the entrance or gathering song. It is easier for them to sing if the song has an easy refrain that can be memorized so that they don't need to be looking at a hymnal or worship aid.

Sign of the Cross and Greeting

After the entrance song, the priest celebrant invites all to make the Sign of the Cross and greets the people with one of the three options provided in the Missal. Because receiving Communion deepens our relationship with Christ, the first option for the greeting is extremely appropriate: "The grace of our Lord Jesus Christ, / and the love of God, / and the communion of the Holy Spirit / be with you all." Following the greeting, he may choose to welcome parents, family, and other visitors and guests, and offer a few words about the Catholic belief in the Eucharist and the importance of what is about to be celebrated. The *Directory for Masses with Children* encourages priest celebrants to speak to the children directly "at the beginning and the end of Mass" so that they "do not feel neglected."[47]

Penitential Act and Kyrie

The Penitential Act is then prayed. This is a time to call to mind our sins and to acknowledge that we are in need of God's mercy and forgiveness. There are three options for the Penitential Act. The first option is the Confiteor, the title coming from the first words "I confess . . . " The second option, probably the least used, is in the form of an antiphonal dialogue between the priest and the assembly. Both these forms are followed by the Kyrie or "Lord, have mercy." The third option, which is the most common, is the brief litany of three invocations that incorporate the Kyrie. The third form is most likely the easiest for the children unless they have memorized the Confiteor or they have easy access to a worship aid where it is printed. The Penitential Act concludes with a prayer of absolution by the priest followed by the Kyrie or "Lord, have mercy."[48] *The Roman Missal* only provides one option for the third form of the Penitential Act. However, the preceding directive notes that the provided text "or other invocations" may be used. This means that parishes may choose to write their own invocations or continue to use one of the eight invocations that were provided in the former Sacramentary. Option VI is perfect for First Communion: "Lord Jesus, you raise us to new life: Lord, have mercy. / Lord Jesus, you forgive us our sins: Christ, have mercy. / Lord Jesus, you feed us with your body and blood: Lord, have mercy." The prayer of absolution follows. Keep in mind that when writing your own invocations, they must be directed to the Lord Jesus and address something he accomplished for our salvation.

---

47 *Directory for Masses with Children*, 17.
48 The Kyrie or "Lord, have mercy" only follows the prayer of absolution if option one or two is used. Option three incorporates the Kyrie into the text.

A good way to think about this is "you" [Lord Jesus] "do" [feed us with your body and blood]. Consider a musical setting of the third option or the Kyrie. Children will especially appreciate singing it in Greek! Be sure to tell them the meaning of the text.

The Blessing and Sprinkling of Water

The Blessing and Sprinkling of Water or Sprinkling Rite may be used instead of the Penitential Act. This rite clearly makes the connection between Baptism and Eucharist and is most appropriate during Christmas Time and Easter Time. It also can be used if First Communion is celebrated on a Saturday or at another time of the year, although it would not be appropriate during Lent.

If the Sprinkling Rite is done, it is wise to prepare the children. Children should already be familiar with blessing themselves with holy water as they enter the church and how this reminds them of their Baptism. Just as they bless themselves with the Sign of the Cross when they dip their fingers in the font so too each child blesses themselves when the priest sprinkles them with holy water during the Sprinkling Rite. If using a Sprinkling Rite, it is appropriate for it to be accompanied by a song focusing on water and Baptism.

Gloria

The Gloria is an ancient hymn of praise to God and should be sung on all Sundays outside of Advent and Lent, and on all solemnities. With the third edition of *The Roman Missal*, the Gloria is also to be sung at ritual Masses celebrated outside of Sunday Mass. Although there is no ritual Mass for First Communion in the Missal as there are for Marriage, Confirmation, and Holy Orders (among others), it is appropriate to also sing the Gloria at the First Communion liturgy. It is recommended that the same setting used at the parish Sunday Mass be used at the First Communion liturgy.

Collect

The Collect follows the Gloria. The text for the prayer is found from the Mass of the day. The assembly may be seated after the Collect.

The Liturgy of the Word

The Liturgy of the Word and the Liturgy of the Eucharist (see below) are the two primary parts of the Mass and are intimately connected. In the Liturgy of the Word, Christ himself, the Word made flesh, is present in the proclamation of Scripture (both Old and New Testament). These ancient and holy texts are traditionally proclaimed form the ambo, the table of the Word—as the altar is the table of the Eucharist.[49] This is where God speaks the truth of salvation to the gathered assembly.

The Readings

If First Communion is celebrated during a regular Sunday parish Mass the readings of the particular Sunday must be used.[50] For example, if First Communion is celebrated during Sunday Mass on the Fourth Sunday of Easter, use the readings from that Sunday as found in the standard *Lectionary for Mass*. You might want to consider the Sunday readings when scheduling the First Communion liturgies in order to emphasize the theology of the Eucharist. If First Communion is celebrated during a Mass apart from the Sunday Mass and takes place during an obligatory solemnity, feast, or memorial, the readings from that day are also used. If First Communion is celebrated at a separate Mass apart from the Mass of the day and the Votive Mass of the Most Holy Eucharist is used, then the parish preparation team may select readings from among the many options for the Most Holy Eucharist found in the Lectionary, #976–981. You might also consider any of the readings from the Ritual Mass for the Initiation of Adults (Apart from the Easter Vigil) at #751–755 in the Lectionary.

Outside of Sunday, only one reading and a Responsorial Psalm are necessary before the Gospel, although two readings may be used. There are a number of Old Testament readings, especially in the Book of Exodus, that prefigure the Eucharist. During Easter Time, you can use a reading from the Acts of the Apostles instead of an Old Testament reading in addition to a reading from the Epistles. The Lectionary provides a special set of New Testament readings from Acts of the Apostles that are to be used during Easter Time if the Mass of the Most Holy Eucharist is used. These are found at #977. Many times "Let the children come to me" (#755.4) is chosen for the Gospel. While this reading evokes sentimental images of children gathering around Jesus, it is not particularly Eucharistic in its theme. The First Communion liturgies are also moments of evangelization and are formative for the entire assembly's Eucharistic spirituality. Choosing a reading that focuses specifically on the Eucharist, such as the Bread of Life passages in John 6 (#981.6–9), or the Story of the Road to Emmaus in Luke (#981.5), might

---

49 See *Lectionary for Mass: Introduction*, 10, and *Built of Living Stones*, 61.
50 This includes the Saturday evening Mass in anticipation of Sunday.

be a better choice. These passages are theologically rich making for excellent homily material for all generations that might be present.

The *Lectionary for Masses with Children* should only be used at Masses primarily for children such as school liturgies, prayer services, and catechetical purposes or if children are dismissed from the main Sunday assembly to participate in a separate Liturgy of the Word. The "Introduction" to the *Lectionary for Masses with Children* notes: "The scriptural readings contained in this Lectionary may be used at Sunday Masses when a large number of children are present along with adults, or when the children have a separate liturgy of the word, or for Masses at which most of the congregation consists of children (e.g., school Masses)."[51] Because the First Communion liturgy is a parish liturgy and consists primarily of adults, it is best to use the standard *Lectionary for Mass*.

The readings should be proclaimed from the ambo.

Responsorial Psalm

Preparation teams must carefully consider the Responsorial Psalm. This proclamation of Scripture "has great liturgical and pastoral importance, since it fosters meditation on the word of God."[52] It is to be sung from the ambo (or other suitable place). Often times, one or several children are asked to recite the psalm as a way to keep them involved in the liturgy. It is not advised to continue this practice. The Responsorial Psalm should be sung by an experienced "psalmist, or 'cantor of the psalm.'"[53] This is a particular liturgical role and the "persons designated for the ministry of psalmist should possess 'the ability for singing and a facility in correct pronunciation and diction.' As one who proclaims the Word, the psalmist should be able to proclaim the text of the Psalm with clarity, conviction, and sensitivity to the text, the music setting, and for those who are listening."[54] This is not to say that the role is restricted to adult cantors. Teens or younger children may serve in this capacity; however, they should be properly trained and formed in this role.

The same criteria for selecting the readings apply to the psalms. However, the seasonal psalms provided in the Lectionary are an additional option (see

---

[51] *Lectionary for Masses with Children: Introduction*, 12.
[52] *General Instruction of the Roman Missal*, 61; see also *Sing to the Lord: Music in Divine Worship*, 115b.
[53] *Sing to the Lord: Music in Divine Worship*, 34.
[54] *Sing to the Lord: Music in Divine Worship*, 35; citing the *General Instruction of the Roman Missal*, 102, and referencing the *Lectionary for Mass*, 56.

Lectionary #173 and 174).[55] Select texts from the seasonal options that are appropriate for the celebration of First Communion. For example, of the four options for Easter, Psalm 66, "Let all the earth cry out to God with joy, alleluia" speaks to the joy of the occasion; and of the nine options for Ordinary Time, Psalm 34, "Taste and see the goodness of the Lord," are perfect options for receiving the Lord.

Homily

The homily is an important part of the Liturgy of the Word. "It should be an explanation of some aspect of the readings from Sacred Scripture or of another text from the Ordinary or from the Proper of the Mass of the day and should take into account both the mystery being celebrated and the particular needs of the listeners."[56] At a First Communion liturgy, many priests take the opportunity to speak to the children directly.[57] Sometimes it becomes a dialogue homily with the priest asking questions or engaging the children in other ways. While these things aren't forbidden, it is important to remember that first communicants are only a small portion of the entire assembly. There are many more adults present and they need to be fed by the homily as well.[58] "When preaching to children is done effectively, the adult hearers are allowed to overhear the Gospel directed to children, but are included as hearers in the process. This type of preaching can never be gimmick ridden or superficial, if it is to be effective."[59] We often underestimate the ability of children to understand and resort to dumbing things down for them. A good homilist can say things to children and still challenge the rest of the assembly.

Profession of Faith

The Profession of Faith or the Creed expresses our core beliefs as Christians. It is required on Sundays, solemnities, and feasts of the Lord. It is usually said on weekdays, although, at First Communion liturgies on days other than Sunday, it would be quite appropriate to recite the Creed. The Nicene Creed or the Apostles' Creed may be used. Because a good number of children may be present at this liturgy, it might be more pastorally appropriate to use the

---

55 See *General Instruction of the Roman Missal*, 61.
56 *General Instruction of the Roman Missal*, 65.
57 See *Directory for Masses with Children*, 19.
58 See *Directory for Masses with Children*, 19.
59 Del Staigers, "Let the Little Children Come to Me: Preaching the Gospel to Children," *Journal of Catholic Education* 4 no. 1 (2000), accessed December 10, 2015, digitalcommons.lmu.edu/ce/vol4/iss1/6.

Apostles' Creed. It is also recommended that the Apostles' Creed is used during Lent and Easter Time to highlight the strong connection in the text to Baptism. Since most First Communion liturgies occur during Easter Time, consider using this version of the Creed.

Parishes might consider the Renewal of Baptismal Promises in place of the Creed. This question and answer format of the Creed is used at celebrations of Baptism, Confirmation, and is included in the Easter Vigil and the liturgies for Easter Sunday. The texts for the Renewal of Baptismal Promises is found in the *Rite of Confirmation*.[60] The rationale of renewing baptismal promises at First Communion liturgies is to make the connection between Eucharist and Baptism. The question is raised, however, whether it is appropriate at a First Communion liturgy. If First Communion is celebrated during Easter Time, everyone, including children, would have or should have already renewed his or her baptismal promises at the Easter Vigil or on Easter Sunday.[61] It would be more appropriate at a First Communion liturgy to begin the liturgy with a Sprinkling Rite especially if the liturgy is celebrated on a Sunday during Easter Time. The children would most likely respond much better to getting wet than to responding to a formula. It would also, as mentioned previously, make the connection for the children of blessing themselves with holy water upon entering the Church. If the First Communion liturgy is celebrated at a separate Mass on a Saturday or other day apart from Sunday, it is best to do the Renewal of Baptismal Promises instead of the Creed.

Universal Prayer

Also called the Prayer of the Faithful, the Universal Prayer is an important part of the liturgy in that it brings to our minds not only our needs but also the needs of the Church, the world, the oppressed, and the local community.[62] It is also a response to the Word of God that we have just heard and serves as a bridge between that Word and the reception of the Eucharist. The petitions may be led by the deacon, a reader, or a cantor at the ambo (or other suitable place). When a deacon is present, he normally leads the petitions.[63] Although many parishes invite first communicants to read the petitions, this

---

60 The Renewal of Baptismal Promises is also found in the *Rite of Confirmation*, 23. At the time of this printing, Confirmation is pending a new English translation.
61 The Renewal of Baptismal Promises on Easter Sunday is an adaptation approved for use in the Dioceses of the United States of America and Canada. See Paul Turner's article, "Water and Promises," *Pastoral Liturgy®* 38, no. 2.
62 See *General Instruction of the Roman Missal*, 68 and 69.
63 See *General Instruction of the Roman Missal*, 71.

should be considered carefully.[64] The response to the petitions can be sung instead of recited. This might help to keep the children focused. A cantor can lead the sung response from the cantor stand while the reader states the petitions from the ambo. Instrumental music can be played softly underneath the spoken petitions. Whether it is sung or recited, the children should be responding in full voice and aware that they are praying for important needs.

Crafting the petitions should be done carefully and not simply be taken from a published book or even from the appendix in the Missal,[65] although these resources can be helpful in writing you own petitions. The petitions follow a pattern. We pray for the Church, the needs of the world, for those who are oppressed, and for the needs of local community. With regard to First Communion celebrations, you do want to include petitions related to the reception of First Communion. If someone in the parish writes the weekly petitions, enlist their help. The important thing is that we do not want all the petitions to focus on the children, when there are so many needs that warrant our prayers.

If First Communion is celebrated at a Sunday Mass, the petitions should be universal, that is, more general, as on any Sunday. Normally the petitions can be adjusted to fit in with the season or focus of the particular Sunday. We do not want to neglect this focus simply because First Communions are being celebrated. Following the petition for the needs of the community, a petition can be added for the first communicants. For example: "For those children among us today who will be receiving our Lord for the first time, and for their parents and catechists who have prepared them."

For First Communion celebrations apart from a Sunday Mass, the same format is followed, however you may be able to tie them in with the celebration. For example:

Church: "For the Church, that through the celebration of the Eucharist, she may continually draw others to Christ." This emphasizes evangelization and our responsibility as Church to lead others to Jesus.

World: "For all world leaders that they may work for peace and justice." Participation in the Eucharist calls us to justice; it obliges us to create "a more human world, a world fully in harmony with God's plan."[66]

---

64 Refer to p. 38 regarding children as liturgical ministers.
65 See Appendix V in *The Roman Missal*.
66 *Ecclesia de Eucharistia*, 20.

Oppressed: "For Catholics living in areas where they are denied access to the Eucharist, and suffer for their faith." This makes the assembly aware of the great gift they have in being able to receive the Eucharist each week, but also of those who cannot.

Local Community: "For our parish community, may we welcome these children to the Eucharistic table for the first time, and continue to help them grow in their faith." We are not only praying for the children now, but for their future, the future of the Church.

Of course these are only examples. Other petitions can be added for parents and catechists, or for other particular needs. It always appropriate to add a petition for the sick and those who have died. If your parish normally announces a particular Mass intention, make sure that you include it in the petitions. You need not have too many petitions. Five or six is usually a good number. The length of the petition need not be very long.

The Liturgy of the Eucharist

The Liturgy of the Eucharist is the second of the two main parts of the Mass. During the Liturgy of the Eucharist, the gathered faithful do what the Lord Jesus himself commanded: to eat and drink his own Body and Blood. The Liturgy of the Eucharist begins with the Preparation of the Gifts, continues with the Eucharistic Prayer, and concludes with the Communion Rite.

Preparation of the Gifts

During the Preparation of the Gifts monetary contributions are collected, the altar is prepared, and members of the liturgical assembly bring forth gifts of bread and wine. Having members of the assembly bring forth the gifts "expresses more clearly the value and meaning of the preparation of the gifts."[67] Along with the bread and wine, we offer all that we are, our joys, and our sorrows to the Lord. We unite our sacrifices to that of Christ's. Many times the first communicants take part in this procession. A catechist or other volunteer should help them retrieve the gifts and cue the children when to process down the center aisle. If the number of children receiving First Communion is too large to have all the children present the gifts, a certain number of children can be chosen to represent the group. If you are trying to avoid feelings of being left out for not being chosen, which often happens,

---

67 *Directory for Masses with Children*, 34.

other members of the assembly might be asked to present the gifts, such as catechists or family members.

The only other gifts that can be presented are gifts for the poor. The gifts for the poor and monetary collections are not to be placed on the altar.[68] Too often, in the name of making the celebration more meaningful, items other than bread and wine, "token items that will be retrieved and returned to ordinary use after the celebration"[69] are brought forward. In some parishes the books the children used in class, projects, personal items, or other objects that might be related to their preparation for the sacrament are included in the procession. Liturgical items such as the chalice, purificators, water cruet, and corporal might also be brought up in some parishes. While this might appear to be helping more children take part in the procession with the gifts, it again puts focus on the children and what they are doing instead of on receiving the Eucharist. The inclusion of such items, although well intentioned, is to be avoided.

Upon processing to the front of the sanctuary with bread and wine, the *General Instruction of the Roman Missal* indicates that the offerings are accepted by the priest or deacon and placed on the altar.[70] The priest and deacon receive our gifts. As such, those carrying the gifts are not to bring the gifts into the sanctuary and place them upon the altar themselves.

A song accompanies the procession with the gifts and the preparation of the altar. Although a choir or an instrumental piece may be used, it is more pastorally appropriate to allow the children the opportunity to sing a song with the assembly. This will also help the children remain focused.

The Eucharistic Prayer and the Acclamations

The Eucharistic Prayer is "the center and high point of the entire celebration."[71] This is our great prayer of thanksgiving to God the Father for all that he has done through Christ by the workings of the Holy Spirit. It is at this time that the offerings of bread and wine become the Body and Blood of Christ. "[T]he meaning of this Prayer is that the whole congregation of the faithful joins itself with Christ in confessing the great deeds of God and in

---

68 See *General Instruction of the Roman Missal*, 73.
69 *Introduction to the Order of the Mass: A Pastoral Resource of the Bishops Committee on the Liturgy*, 105.
70 *General Instruction of the Roman Missal*, 73, 75.
71 *General Instruction of the Roman Missal*, 78.

the offering of Sacrifice. The Eucharistic Prayer requires that everybody listen to it with reverence and in silence."[72]

It is so important that the children are engaged in this prayer, but not at the expense of good liturgical principles. In an effort to involve the children, some priests will invite the children to come into the sanctuary and stand around the altar. Think for a moment about what this conveys. It is singling out specific members of the assembly who are not ministers of the liturgy to enter the sanctuary. Often, the children aren't paying that much attention to the actions of the priest, but are looking around at the vessels and the Missal on the altar, glancing back at family members, talking to each other, fidgeting, and so on. While parents might think it is cute and special, the children might distract others in the assembly who are trying to focus. It takes away from the sacredness of the Eucharistic Prayer and what is occurring. Bringing the children around the altar often turns into a photo opportunity with people holding up smart phones when they should be attentive to the consecration of the Eucharist.

It is the norm for the Dioceses of the United States for the assembly to kneel during the Eucharistic Prayer from the Sanctus until after the Amen and then after the Lamb of God.[73] Because of this directive, it is best for children to remain in their pews and kneel with the rest of the assembly. "A common bodily posture, to be observed by all those taking part, is a sign of the unity of the members of the Christian community gathered together for the Sacred Liturgy, for it expresses the intentions and spiritual attitude of the participants and also fosters them."[74]

Before beginning the Eucharistic Prayer, the priest can mention to the children the importance of this prayer and ask them to pay special attention.

The Eucharistic Prayer includes three acclamations that are sung by the entire assembly: the Holy, Memorial Acclamation, and the Amen. There are three options for the Memorial Acclamation. Consider using the text "When we eat this Bread and drink this Cup, / we proclaim your Death, O Lord, / until you come again" if there is a familiar setting in your parish repertoire. This is not the time to introduce new acclamations or Mass settings. With regard to acclamations, since there likely will be many guests from out of the

---

[72] *General Instruction of the Roman Missal*, 78.
[73] See *General Instruction of the Roman Missal*, 43.
[74] *General Instruction of the Roman Missal*, 42.

parish, using popular acclamations that are common to most parishes increases participation.

The Communion Rite

The Communion Rite is the last part of the Liturgy of the Eucharist and includes the Our Father, Sign of Peace, Lamb of God, reception of Communion, and the Prayer after Communion. The Our Father may be sung. Consider this option only if it is regularly done in your parish, especially since there will be many visitors. Use a familiar setting for the Lamb of God. The *Rite of Christian Initiation of Adults* notes that it would be appropriate for the priest celebrant to remind everyone about "the preeminence of the eucharist"[75] before praying the Lamb of God.

The Communion Procession and Reception of First Communion

The procession to receive Communion is a liturgical procession and a sign of unity of the gathered community moving forward to receive Christ and to become what they have received. A song accompanies this ritual and it should begin as the priest receives.[76] Enough music should be prepared so that the assembly has the opportunity to sing while everyone receives. If more than one song is selected it is best to provide an instrumental transition from one to the next, rather than as two separate pieces. This helps to musically unify the action that is taking place. Familiar Eucharistic songs with simple refrains are best so that everyone, including the children, can sing without looking at a book or worship aid. In other words, a song where people can sing and walk at the same time!

The logistics of the Communion procession depends upon the children's seating arrangement. If the children are seated with their family, there are several options:

The parents alone can accompany the children and receive with them. This option works well when the children are seated with their parents although it can be difficult when the entire family is seated in the row. Also having the parents accompany the children to receive allows the parents to help the children who happen to forget in their excitement what they rehearsed with regard to how to receive Communion and how to get back to their seat.

---

75 *Rite of Christian Initiation of Adults*, 243. This directive is specific to those receiving full initiation at the Easter Vigil; however, it can also be applied to First Communion with children.

76 See *General Instruction of the Roman Missal*, 86.

The entire family can exit the row to receive with the child leading their family forward. This is how families would receive Communion at a regular Sunday Mass. While the focus is not on just the children receiving at this time it keeps the family together.

All the children alone, who are seated at the ends of each row, can receive first and then the rest of the families. This arrangement might need a bit of logistical planning as to how the children get back to their seat. It seems obvious that they would simply walk around and sit at the other end until the rest of the row receives, but it is easier said than done. The children can also process single file and return to their exact place, but then the rest of the row would have to climb over the child in order to receive.

If the children are seated in the common arrangement of children only, then it is natural that they receive first without their parents. It would be helpful to have ushers, hospitality ministers, or someone else nearby to assist the children if they are confused after they receive as to what they are to do or where they are to go next.

There are several ways for the Communion procession to take place. Children may come forward with their parents.

Catechists and hospitality ministers should be present during the Communion procession to help children, their families, and the rest of the assembly know when to come forward.

When children come forward they may hold their hands either in the traditional posture of prayer with palms and fingertips together or else in a folded position, if this is the common practice in their parish.[77] Before approaching the minister of Communion, a sign of reverence is called for. In the United States, this sign is a bow of the head.[78] The sign of reverence

---

77 See p. 68.
78 See *General Instruction of the Roman Missal*, 160.

Preparing the First Communion Liturgy

should not take place while the person in front of them is receiving. Instead, the child should wait to make the sign of reverence until after they have approached the Communion minister. After the sign of reverence, the Communion minister should say, "The Body (or Blood) of Christ" and the child responds, "Amen" or the communicant can bow their head while saying "Amen." The same sign of reverence is made before receiving from the cup if the parish practices receiving from both species.[79]

The *Rite of Christian Initiation of Adults* emphasizes that "it is most desirable that [all] receive communion under both kinds."[80] Although this directive is specific to adult initiation, it is good guidance for the First Communion liturgy. The practice of receiving the Precious Blood from the cup should be practiced in all parishes. According to the *General Instruction of the Roman Missal*, "Holy Communion has a fuller form as a sign when it takes place under both kinds. For in this form the sign of the Eucharistic banquet is more clearly evident and clearer expression is given to the divine will by which the new and eternal Covenant is ratified in the Blood of the Lord."[81] There is no reason why a child cannot receive from the cup. Many parents are concerned about the use of alcohol, but it is important to remember that the child is not drinking more than a small sip. Most children do not like the taste of wine, so they only touch it with their lips. Others might be concerned about germs passed from using a common Communion cup. The chance of catching something from sharing the cup is very minimal as wiping the rim between each communicant, the turning of the cup, and the alcohol

The cup may be ministered to children.

---

79 See p. 68 regarding directions for receiving in the hand and on the tongue.
80 *Rite of Christian Initiation of Adults*, 243.
81 *General Instruction of the Roman Missal*, 281.

content of the wine makes passing germs unlikely. It is wise, however, that if an adult or child has a cold, or if there are cases of the flu or other communicable disease in the family home, they should refrain from receiving from the cup. While receiving both species might be encouraged in a parish, parents do have the right to decline to have their children partake of the Precious Blood.

In the United States, the normative way for receiving Communion is standing.[82] However, there are some parishes that do continue to practice kneeling at an altar rail. The pastor determines the posture the children will assume at their First Communion. If the children will be kneeling, no additional sign of reverence is required. It is important to note, that even though standing is the norm in most parishes, no one can be refused Communion if they choose to kneel.[83] In order to keep order and avoid confusing the children, their posture should be uniform, at least for their First Communion.

Upon returning to their place after receiving, the children should be encouraged to continue singing the Communion song. Many suggest that this is a time to quietly pray, but as long as the communion procession is continuing we sing as a sign of our union with each other in Christ. After everyone has received there should be a period of silence for personal prayer. Children should be encouraged to thank Christ for the gift of the Eucharist. A song of praise may follow.

The Concluding Rites

The Concluding Rites are a call to service and mission. The final blessing and dismissal to "Go, glorifying the Lord by your life," commissions the assembly to take what they have heard (Word) and received (Eucharist) into the world, so that the world may be changed just as we are changed during the liturgy.

Following the Prayer after Communion it is appropriate for the priest to offer a few concluding remarks to the children and the assembly. Although this is not a time to give out certificates or gifts, have the children sing a song, or do anything else that is not part of the liturgy, the priest might lead the assembly in congratulating the children. The priest celebrant may also use this time to thank everyone who was involved in First Communion catechesis, formation, and liturgy preparation. If a parish reception follows the liturgy, now is the time to provide necessary details.

---

82 See *General Instruction of the Roman Missal*, 160.
83 *Redemptionis sacramentum*, 91.

A closing song may accompany the closing procession. Eucharistic themes and the call to service should be the focus of the text.

The children can be part of the closing procession or they can remain in their seats. If the children do process, be sure to gather them in a place with adult supervision following the liturgy where their parents can meet them. Many parishes have them gather for a group picture at this time.

Preparing a Worship Aid

In order to help people feel welcome and able to participate, a worship aid for the First Communion liturgy is very useful—especially if there are visitors who are new to the parish or are not Catholic. A worship aid also serves as a keepsake of this important occasion as well as encouraging participation. If a worship aid is created, the parish staff will need to discuss whose responsibility it will be to prepare them. They are easy to design and templates are available to help make the task simpler. Once a template is made it can be used year after year. If desired, decorative covers for the worship aid can be ordered or designed by someone in the parish. When creating a worship aid, the primary goal should be providing the assembly the means to participate with the responses, music, gestures, and posture. Even if First Communion takes place during Sunday Mass and the parish is familiar with the Mass responses and a common musical repertoire, there will still be many visitors and guests present. Do your best to ensure that they will know how to respond! Be sure that the worship aid is easy to read and follow. Use headings for the various parts of the Mass and clearly mark the various roles and responses. Also note when to stand, kneel, sit, or bow, when necessary. You need not include the full texts of the readings unless there will be hearing impaired present or the liturgy is bilingual. Ideally, the assembly will be provided with the music printed in the worship aid rather than hymnal number references. This will avoid confusion and the need to change resources throughout the liturgy. It is important to note that most music, except that which is in the public domain, is copyrighted, and obtaining permission to print music is a matter of justice. In this way, the rights of the composer to compensation for the printing of his or her music are protected. Contact the publisher well in advance of printing the worship aid to get permission and pay any fees that may be incurred. Do not forget to put the copyright information in the worship aid as well. Many parishes purchase a service that provides a license and permission to print music from specific or multiple publishers. If the parish subscribes to these services any other permission does not need to be obtained, but the copyright information and license number must be printed in the worship aid.[84] Music graphics such as PDFs or JPGs are often available with this subscription. These can be easily inserted into the worship aid and does not require the former methods of cutting, pasting, and taping.

Provide the assembly worship aids.

Since there will be visitors and guests, it is recommended to reprint the guidelines for receiving Communion.[85] There may be relatives and friends in attendance who are not Catholic or who are not regularly practicing Catholics. They are often unaware of Catholic teaching on receiving Communion. Printing these guidelines helps to avoid confusion and also provides catechesis about the sacrament.[86]

Make sure enough worship aids are printed for the number of people you are expecting to attend. While people can share, it is good for participation if everyone has their own worship aid.

Printing the names of the children in the worship aid is a good idea as it can also be used as a keepsake for the families. If there are multiple First Communion liturgies on one day, print all the names of the children in the worship aid. If it is not possible to print the names of the children in the worship aid, consider printing them in the Sunday bulletin. A prayer for the children could be included for parishioners to pray at home. If First

---

84 Reprint permission for the main Catholic music publishers may be obtained through www.onelicense.net (GIA Music and Liturgical Press), www.licensingonline.org/en-us (Oregon Catholic Press), and www.wlp.jspaluch.com/3396.htm (World Library Publications).

85 The "Guidelines for the Reception of Holy Communion" may be found on the United States Conference of Catholic Bishops' website: http://www.usccb.org/prayer-and-worship/the-mass/order-of-mass/liturgy-of-the-eucharist/guidelines-for-the-reception-of-communion.cfm.

86 *Redemptionis sacramentum* states: "Furthermore when Holy Mass is celebrated for a large crowd—for example, in large cities—care should be taken lest out of ignorance non-Catholics or even non-Christians come forward for Holy Communion, without taking into account the Church's Magisterium in matters pertaining to doctrine and discipline. It is the duty of Pastors at an opportune moment to inform those present of the authenticity and the discipline that are strictly to be observed" (84).

Communion is on several Sundays, worship aids will need to be provided for each Mass or, for simplicity, a generic aid could be used on those occasions with just the Mass parts and common music.

Parish Policies

Attire

It is customary in many places for little girls and boys to dress in white dresses, veils, suits, and ties. Parents of girls especially look forward to dressing their daughters as little "brides," sometimes spending great sums of money on elaborate dresses and veils, shoes, hair, flowers, and even makeup. But is this kind of dress necessary for receiving the sacrament? The answer is no. While it is a very special day for families, there is no requirement for how the children dress. Each parish may however, establish guidelines for how they would like the children to be dressed for First Communion. The white dress and veil for girls, and dark suit and tie might be an established tradition in your parish. It might even be a cultural tradition. Some cultures may include flowers in girls' hair instead of veils. It is important to take these traditions into consideration when setting parish policy on a dress code for First Communion.

It has been suggested that the white dress relates to Baptism and initiation. Paul Turner disputes this, along with the idea of it representing the eschatological wedding banquet, or the dress of the angels:

> [T]he First Communion dress [does not] contribute to initiatory symbolism. Some have argued that the dress is baptismal in origin, but this does not fit the creation of the ceremony or the variation in the color of the boys clothing. The veil and the dress of girls, reminiscent of a bridal gown, has led to interpretations of participating in the Eucharist as in the eschatological wedding banquet; if so, it made more sense when the participants were adolescents and when Communion was infrequent. Some early witnesses call the outfit the dress of angels—probably angels who adore the real presence of God, not who receive Communion. If nothing else, the dress seems to represent formality in its origin and tradition ever since. It symbolizes First Communion, not baptism. The dress does not effectively connect the sacrament with initiation.[87]

---

[87] Paul Turner, *Ages of Initiation: The First Two Christian Millennia* (Collegeville, MN: The Liturgical Press, 2000), p. 62.

The wearing of a veil is most likely a holdover from the time, in the not-too-distant past, when girls and women were required to wear head coverings in church. Looking at old photographs of First Communion from the early to middle last century, you can see a variety of head coverings for First Communion. Girls wore veils, hats, wreaths of flowers, or large bows. It is no longer required for females to wear a head covering, but the tradition is strong in some areas.

Some parishes while specifying a white dress or a suit might also set policies such as not allowing girls' dresses that are sleeveless, strapless, or of a specific length. Some may limit the color of boys' suits. While this might create a certain uniformity and even formality to the occasion, a specific type of clothing is not required.

There was a time in the not-too-distant past, when girls and women would wear gloves as a matter of etiquette. Young girls would receive gloves in their First Communion kits along with rosaries and missals. For the most part, wearing gloves is not in fashion, except to keep hands warm in cold climates, but parents still like to see their daughters wearing bright white gloves on First Communion day. It lends a bit more formality to the occasion but can present a problem when it comes to receiving Communion. In the past when Communion was received at the altar rail and on the tongue, gloves were not a concern. Today, however, with the reception of Communion in the hand, wearing gloves to receive would not be appropriate. While there is no documentation that forbids the practice of wearing gloves, it is only proper to receive the host in bare hands as any cloth that touches the host is to be treated in a specific way with regard to laundering, in case there are any fragments attached to the cloth. Many parishes simply ask girls not to wear gloves while others allow them to be worn in processions in and out of church but not in the Communion procession. However since some girls might forget to take them off it is best to not allow gloves.

Since no specific dress is required, girls might be asked to wear a nice dress (it does not have to be white), and boys to wear neat slacks, a jacket, or a nice shirt and tie. Any dress code requirement must take into consideration there might be families that cannot afford to purchase the required or suggested clothing. Especially in poorer parishes it might be very difficult for parents to purchase special attire for their children. In some cases, parishioners can be asked to "dress" a first communicant, purchasing special dresses or suits and shoes for families in need. Collecting gently used Communion clothes and having them available for families is another possibility.

Other parishes encourage children to wear an alb. Although the alb is most often worn by liturgical ministers, it is a baptismal garment and proper to all the baptized. Wearing this garment not only reminds the children and the assembly of Baptism, and the reception of Eucharist as a Sacrament of Initiation, it ensures uniformity of dress and takes the emphasis off elaborate clothing choices. Whatever a parish decides to do regarding attire, no child should be denied the sacrament or made to feel ostracized because of their clothing.

Photography

Photography is always a question that arises when a parish has any sacramental celebration. Of course parents want to have a photograph or record this special occasion in their child's life. Today, with smart phones and small video recorders, it is so much easier to be able to snap a photo or record a video at a moment's notice. Problems occur when a large number of parents or family or professional photographers are clamoring for photos during the liturgy.

Most parishes have established rules or guidelines for photographers and videographers during liturgies. It is important that upon establishing guidelines that the parents are made aware of them long before the First Communion Mass. If this is not communicated, you run the risk of parents hiring professional photographers only to be told the day of First Communion that this practice is not allowed. There will be unhappy parents who will probably be expressing anger at the DRE, liturgist, music director, or pastor. Knowing rules ahead of time avoids these problems.

Distraction and disruption are the main concern with photographers. In order to alleviate this problem and be sensitive to the needs of parents, parishes can hire a photographer, and perhaps a videographer as well, to take pictures and record the liturgy. This photographer can stand in a discrete position and take photos of each child receiving. Digital recordings can be inexpensively made into DVDs for families. The cost of these services can be figured into any sacramental preparation fees the parish might require, or parents can choose to purchase them from the photographers.

Parishes that allow professional photographers should have clear and succinct guidelines with regard to where photographers can stand during the liturgy, when they can and cannot take pictures or videos, and whether or not they are allowed to use a flash or other lighting. Parishes must also set guidelines if they allow parents and guests to take photos or videos. Those taking photos should be asked to remain in their seats when taking photos and to not use a flash. An announcement should be made before Mass begins with regard to taking photographs, reminding those in the assembly of the reverence that should be displayed during the liturgy. Limiting photographs to the entrance and recessional processions is another good way to face the photography issue. Taking a group photo on the church lawn or having a professional available for individual portrait photographs in the parish hall following the liturgy or at another time, are other ways to provide for the need for photos of the children.

Parish Documentation of First Communion

It is important to keep records of the children's reception of the sacraments. While it is not universally required to keep records of First Communion in a parish register, most dioceses require it and keep the register with other sacramental registers in the rectory or parish office.[88] Recording information accurately is very important. Adequate records are necessary in the event that a child is transferring to another parish or stops attending religious education classes. It is not necessary to notify the parish where the child was baptized that he or she received First Communion, although some parishes might choose to do so. In the event that a parish does not have a First Communion register, it is important that records of First Communion and the Sacrament of Reconciliation are recorded. Permanent record cards might be kept in the Religious Education Office. These cards are very helpful and include information such as Baptism and Confirmation dates. Some parishes also keep records in the parish census, recording sacramental information for all family members. This information should be accessible in the event that proof of receiving a sacrament is necessary in the future.

Accurate records for each child include the date of Baptism and the church where it occurred. In order to do this it is essential that copies of the baptismal certificates for the children be collected as part of the registration procedure for children entering a religious education program. The reason

---

[88] The *Code of Canon Law* only requires that "each parish is to have parochial registers, that is, those of baptisms, marriages, deaths, and others as prescribed by the conference of bishops or the diocesan bishop. The pastor is to see to it that these registers are accurately inscribed and carefully preserved" (Canon 535 §1).

for this is that today, many parents do not necessarily bring their child for Baptism, or they might have had their child baptized in a Protestant church. While most Christian Baptisms are validly celebrated, the child will still need to be received into the Catholic Church, and this too must be accurately recorded in the parish register.[89] Sometimes the fact that children have not been baptized in a Catholic parish is missed because the person collecting the baptismal certificate did not read it correctly. Parish secretaries need to receive instruction on how to read baptismal certificates in order that any problems with regard to Baptism can be uncovered early, and the situation can be dealt with in a timely manner.

The Protection of Children

The protection of children is at the forefront of any parish ministry where children or any other vulnerable persons are involved. In compliance with the United States Bishops' 2002 *Charter for Protection of Children and Young People*, all dioceses have child protection programs in place for adults working with children.[90] These mandatory workshops help adults learn to recognize the signs of possible child sexual abuse and other types of abuse as well. VIRTUS® is a nationwide organization that is utilized by many dioceses.[91] Trained local facilitators run these workshops, and participants who work with children receive frequent Internet updates. While VIRTUS® is the most popular, there are other programs utilized by dioceses that serve the same purpose. All dioceses have policies in place for reporting suspected child abuse. Check with your diocesan office responsible for child protection for programs and for more information on requirements for adults working with children. These programs are not only for catechists but also for all parish volunteers who will be working with and in the vicinity of children, such as hospitality ministers, choir directors, and those who work preparing the liturgies. Many parishes mandate these programs for all parish volunteers as a way of helping to ensure that all children in the parish will be safe from abuse.

---

89 A child only needs to be received into full Communion if they were validly baptized in another Christian tradition and seek Communion and Confirmation within the Catholic Church. The "Rite of Reception of Baptized Christians into the Full Communion of the Catholic Church" as found in the *Rite of Christian Initiation of Adults* should be used (see 473–504 in the rite).

90 The charter is available on the United States Bishops' website: www.usccb.org/issues-and-action/child-and-youth-protection/charter.cfm.

91 See their website: www.virtus.org/virtus/.

It is also important that adults working with children establish certain boundaries with regard to physical contact with children and also with regard to not being alone with a child. Communications via e-mail or social media without parental permission or knowledge is also to be avoided. While this would not necessarily be a problem with children of First Communion age, it is still important to be aware of communication boundaries in all your communications, especially if you are involved in ministry as you are held to a higher standard and do represent the parish.

Another area where you need to be careful with regard to protecting children is with the use of photographs or videos of the children, especially if the photos or videos will be uploaded to the parish website, social media site, or in the parish bulletin. You will need to have parental permission to use any photos or videos of children. Many religious education programs and schools include a photo use permission form as part of the yearly registration form. If the parish is hiring a photographer for First Communion, care must be taken that the photographer or videographer is aware that he or she may not use the pictures for any other purpose other than to provide them to have them available for parents to purchase or for parish use. Most parents are happy to provide permission to post pictures and videos on the parish website or bulletin, however it is prudent not to include the names of the children or any other identifiable or sensitive information about the children. It is unfortunate we live in a time where these precautions are necessary, especially in a religious setting. But part of being a good Christian is to work to protect the most vulnerable among us.

Other Issues

In the Catholic Church, only validly baptized Catholics who are properly prepared and disposed are permitted to receive Communion. There are a few extraordinary exceptions to this but they do not particularly pertain to the topic of First Communion for children. There are situations whereby parents request that their children be initiated into the Catholic Church and thus receive First Communion. The *Rite of Christian Initiation of Adults* should be used in these circumstances. Part II of this rite includes the Christian initiation of children who have reached the catechetical age.

Unbaptized Children of Catechetical Age

On occasion, a family comes into the parish school or religious education program with a child or children who have not received Baptism. According to the *Rite of Christian Initiation of Adults* and Canon Law, children of catechetical age, that is, at or beyond the age of reason, who are becoming members of the Catholic Church, are considered adults.[92] These children are to be prepared to receive all three Sacraments of Initiation, Baptism, Confirmation, and Eucharist, in that order, at the same Mass, usually at the Easter Vigil.

Children Who Have Been Baptized in Other Christian Faiths

You may have children in the parish who were baptized in another Christian community and now wish to be received into the Catholic Church. It is important to note that, barring a few exceptions, most Christian Baptisms are valid and accepted in the Catholic Church as long as the Baptism occurred with water (proper matter) and the Trinitarian formula (proper form). It often happens that the parents are baptized Catholics but for some reason or another baptized their child in a different faith community. This is why it is so important to examine all children's baptismal certificates to ensure that they indeed were baptized in a Catholic Church before preparing for First Communion. In cases where a child was not baptized in a Catholic Church, the process of formation for reception into the Church needs to be determined on an individual basis according to their particular needs. They should not be included in the catechumenate with unbaptized children, except perhaps for common catechetical sessions that might also include their Catholic peers. However, they are to receive specific preparation for and celebrate the Sacrament of Reconciliation some time before being received into the Church. Upon further preparation, they make a Profession of Faith and receive Confirmation and Eucharist at the same Mass, even though their peers might not be receiving Confirmation until a later age.[93] "The reception of candidates into the communion of the Catholic Church should ordinarily take place at the Sunday Eucharist of the parish community, in such a way that it is understood that they are indeed Christian believers who have already shared in the sacramental life of the Church and are now welcomed into the Catholic Eucharistic community upon their profession of faith and confirmation, if

---

92 See *Rite of Christian Initiation of Adults*, part 2, chap. 1; *National Statues for the Catechumenate*, 18; *Code of Canon Law*, 97 §1, 99, 852 §1.
93 See *National Statutes for the Catechumenate*, 30–37.

they have not been confirmed, before receiving the eucharist."[94] It's preferable that this not take place during the Easter Vigil.

Children Baptized in an Eastern Rite

The Eastern Rite refers to those Churches that follow the rites established in the Middle East, Eastern Europe, Africa, and other areas of the East. Eastern Rite Churches are divided into a) those who are in union with Rome, called Eastern Rite Catholic Churches, and b) those who are not in union with Rome called Orthodox or Oriental Churches. The term Eastern Catholic Churches refers to the twenty-three autonomous or *sui iuris* Churches who accept the pope as the head of the Church. Eastern Rite Churches usually celebrate all three Sacraments of Initiation together. Children baptized into an Eastern Rite Catholic Church are members of the Catholic Church. Thus a child baptized in an Eastern Rite Church, with a few exceptions, has most likely already received their First Communion. Parents who are Eastern Rite, both those in union with Rome and those who are not, may choose to send their children to our parish schools. Of course in Catholic school, children are prepared to receive First Communion. It is inappropriate to include Eastern Rite Catholic children in the liturgies of First Communion with the other children. Doing so negates that they have already been welcomed to the table. Parents of children baptized Eastern Rite Catholics need to know early on that their children, if attending a Latin Rite parish and participating in a Latin Rite Mass, can receive Communion at any Mass they participate in, even before the age of reason if they received Communion at Baptism. The same would be true for children baptized in an Orthodox Church who have become Catholic (although they would not be admitted to a Latin Rite but to the Eastern Rite Catholic Church that corresponds to their Orthodox Church). Contact the chancellor of the diocese for more information.

At times the parents of these children might insist that it is unfair that their child cannot participate in the First Communion Mass with their peers. It is important that the pastor or catechetical leader empathetically discuss with the parents that the child is not being denied Communion. If First Communion is celebrated at a Sunday parish Mass, there is no reason why the child cannot attend and receive as part of the assembly, but they should not participate in a way that suggests this is their First Communion. It is also

---

94 *National Statutes for the Catechumenate*, 32.

important to note that the manner of receiving Communion differs in the Eastern Rite. Eastern Rite Catholics used leavened bread. This bread is placed on a spoon and dipped into the consecrated wine. This might be confusing to a child.

The Bishops' Committee on the Relationship between Eastern and Latin Catholic Churches wrote in 1999, "Holy Communion may be received in any Catholic Church. Since sacramental initiation in the mystery of salvation is perfected in the reception of the Divine Eucharist, children of Eastern Catholic Churches who have not received the Eucharist at the time of their Christian initiation should receive their first Holy Communion in their own autonomous Church."[95] This seems to indicate that in some churches there is the possibility that Communion was not received at Baptism. If this is so, and there are no churches of their particular rite in the area, then they can receive First Communion within the Latin Rite.

Children of Eastern Orthodox Churches are not eligible for Communion in Catholic Churches. The conditions for rare exceptions can be found in the *Directory for the Application of Principles and Norms on Ecumenism*, 131.

Parish Receptions Following First Communion

Families love to have celebrations following important moments in their children's lives, and First Communion, for many families, is one of those moments. The problem occurs, unfortunately, when the celebration following the reception of the sacrament overshadows the experience of receiving the Lord in the Eucharist for the first time. This misplaced focus is most evident with regard to the Sacrament of Matrimony, where the reception is so primary that the celebration of the sacrament has become insignificant.

We see this trend—the focus on the party—with First Communion as well. While it is true that First Communion is a significant moment in the life of a Catholic child, for some families, elaborate parties, which can be compared to a small wedding reception, overshadow the reception of the sacrament. Parents spend thousands of dollars for such receptions and when children are asked what was special about the day of their First Communion, they respond the party, the gifts, or the dress for girls. Rarely do they speak

---

[95] United States Conference of Catholic Bishops, *Eastern Catholics in the United States of America* (Washington, DC: USCCB Publishing, 1999), p. 28–29.

about receiving Christ. These receptions also may cause negative feelings among those parents that cannot afford to host such parties for their children.

Parents can be encouraged to put the proper emphasis on receiving the Eucharist rather than having a big party, but the truth is, we like to celebrate. A simple backyard party or family dinner is a great way to celebrate the day. In order to mark the day and celebrate as a parish community, some parishes have attempted to combat the big reception trend by hosting their own reception in the parish hall following the First Communion Mass. This is usually easier to accomplish in smaller parishes where all the children receive at the same Mass. Parishes that offer hospitality after each of their regular Sunday liturgies, and celebrate First Communions at a Sunday parish Mass, can provide a special cake and invite the children and their families to attend along with the rest of the parishioners attending that Mass. This helps form community, especially among those families who may not attend Mass each week.

Large parishes that have multiple First Communion Masses over several weeks can host a Communion breakfast on a Sunday a week or two after all the children have received First Communion. The children can dress in their First Communion dresses and celebrate all together. Some parishes that have all First Communion Masses before the end of May might combine a Communion breakfast with a parish May crowning. After Mass the first communicants lead a procession to a statue of the Blessed Virgin Mary and a crown of flowers is placed on the statue. During the parish reception is also a good opportunity to invite the children to sing a special song they learned in religion class or to display banners or other projects they may have completed in class as they prepared to receive Communion. Parish receptions are also an opportune time for parish fellowship and to welcome families back to church, and also be a way to evangelize.[96] Providing these opportunities also provides celebratory outreach to those families that could not afford a party or had few family and guests to celebrate their child's First Communion.

---

96 See p. 26.

Frequently Asked Questions

There are many questions concerning the reception of First Communion. The purpose of this section is to provide answers concerning primarily liturgical or ritual issues. For questions concerning other issues, especially those related to the *Code of Canon Law*, please consult with your pastor and/or (arch)diocesan offices.

1. What is the purpose of the First Communion certificate?

Unlike the baptismal certificate which is proof of Baptism and also contains records of Confirmation, Holy Orders, and Marriages, a First Communion certificate is more of a keepsake. Parishes may present these to the children in order that the parents can have a remembrance and personal record of the day. As with any sacramental certificates, they are not formally presented to the children at Mass. To do so takes away from the liturgical celebration and can make it appear as if receiving First Communion is an achievement, not a gift of the Lord that they have just received. If certificates are given out, it is best to distribute them after Mass or mail them home to the parents. Another nice option is to present them to all those children at a Communion breakfast or First Communion celebration party.

2. Other than the renewal of baptismal promises or the sprinkling rite, how does the liturgy itself help to emphasize that Communion is a Sacrament of Initiation and connected to Baptism?

It often appears that since the reordering of the Sacraments of Initiation, that is, in allowing Communion to be received before Confirmation, the connection with initiation has deteriorated, at least when it comes to children. Paul Turner writes, "First Communion rituals exhibit a self-concept not of initiation or even of communion with God and the Church, but of attainment of a catechetical level and of privatized devotion to the Eucharist."[1] We have discussed ways to connect Eucharist to Baptism through the renewal of

---

1 *Ages of Initiation*, p. 61.

Baptismal promises, the sprinkling rite, or use of the Apostles' Creed instead of the Nicene Creed. The priest or deacon could make the connection with Baptism in his homily or in opening remarks, explaining simply how Eucharist is a Sacrament of Initiation and tying it in with Baptism. A petition in the Universal Prayer can mention the parents "who first brought their children to the font and now continue their formation toward full initiation by bringing them to receive the Eucharist." Encourage families to invite the child's godparents to attend if they are available.

3. How can the whole parish be a part of the First Communion process?

Since we have been talking about First Communion as being a parish event, it is important to include the entire parish in some way during the time of preparation. There will be a number of parishioners who of course will volunteer to be catechists or to help with preparation in other ways, but what about the parish at large, how can they be part of this joyous event? The best way is to have the parish pray for the children and their families. The First Communion children should be mentioned in the Universal Prayer at specific times during their preparation, but especially when they are about to receive First Reconciliation and First Communion. Some parishes include the children's names on the prayer ministry list, or ask parishioners to take a child's name that has been printed on a card and to pray for that child during the time of preparation. For safety's sake, it is best to only print the child's first name and no other personal information. There are some parishes that print the children's names in the bulletin or place pictures of the children who are receiving First Communion on a poster or on the website in order that people can see who is preparing to receive. It is important to always get permission from the parents before posting any pictures of children and never to put names with their picture.

Another idea would be to invite parishioners, especially older ones, to attend one of the classes and to talk to the children about what it was like when they received First Communion. Children love to hear a story of what is was like "in the old days," and people love telling their stories. Parishioners can also be asked to volunteer to help out at a First Communion retreat, or to prepare and host a post-Communion breakfast. Encourage parishioners to congratulate the children after Mass during the weeks following First

Communion. Encouraging the children to wear their communion outfits makes spotting them easy.

Let's not leave out the older children. Those in the other grade levels can design cards for the first communicants that can be delivered to them following First Communion. You can ask the older children to pray for the first communicants during prayer time in class and encourage them to pray for them at home as well. Getting the whole parish involved makes First Communion season special and exciting, encourages participation in the parish, and helps parents to feel welcomed and affirmed.

4. Can children help prepare the liturgy?

If the number of children in the parish receiving First Communion is small, it might be beneficial to allow the children to assist in preparing the liturgy for their First Communion. Too large a group will elicit too many opinions and ideas. However, a small group of children can be selected to join in the preparation in various ways. One might think that it is ridiculous to have children help in preparation, as they are so young. This involvement of children with the preparation will only work well if the children have been attending Mass and are familiar with the flow of the liturgy through their participation, and how well they have been engaged in liturgical celebrations.

There are many things children can do to help prepare the liturgy. Their input is helpful as they might be aware of things that adults overlook. Robert Piercy writes, "As you prepare to work with the children you'll need to enter into an attitude of wonder at the children's response to God."[2] There are many different areas where the children can be involved. Piercy lists six:

Listening and discussing the readings:

Although the pastor, liturgist, or DRE might choose the readings, children can certainly discuss the readings and engage in a form of *lectio divina* (prayerful reflection on the readings) to see how the readings speak to them. Their thoughts and reflections might be helpful to the priest or deacon in preparing a homily.

Helping select music:

Simply asking children what songs they might want to sing at their First Communion could elicit selections from the latest Disney film to the most

---

2 Robert Piercy, *Preparing Masses with Children: 15 Easy Steps* (Chicago: Liturgy Training Publications, 2012), p. 5.

recent pop hit. Music is such an integral part of the liturgy that choosing the right music should be left to the professionals. Nevertheless, if the children are used to signing certain songs or hymns at Mass, and seem to have a preference for a particular one, they could be asked if they would like that song sung at First Communion. The parish music director should be a part of these conversations and could lead the children in singing a number of selections during a religious education class. If a number of hymns and songs are being considered, the children can be asked which ones they like the best. In this way the children feel a sense of being part of the preparations and they will most likely be more apt to participate in the singing. Once the hymn is chosen, go over the lyrics with the children—not just to memorize them, but also to truly understand what they mean. In other words, to teach the children that hymns are a form of praying.

Assisting in writing the Universal Prayer (Prayer of the Faithful):
Piercy offers excellent guidelines for writing the Universal Prayer with input from the children. Remember that the intercessions follow a specific formula given to us by the Church:

- "for the needs of the Church;
- for public authorities and the salvation of the whole world;
- for those burdened by any kind of difficulty;
- for the local community."[3]

When preparing the intercessions with the children, ask them to reflect upon the readings that have been chosen for the liturgy, and to pick out any themes or words that might help them in formulating intercessions. If children have been accustomed to voicing petitions in class, they might have many personal needs, such as an ill parent or a deceased relative that they want to include. In such situations one general intercession that includes all the ill or deceased relatives and friends of the First Communion families is sufficient to cover all their needs.

Input on the liturgical environment:
Children can help prepare the space by creating banners. If large handcrafted banners are used in the parish for First Communion, choose some children to help design and craft them. Popular First Communion pew banners are an easy way to have all the children involved, but there is a disadvantage in

---

3   *General Instruction of the Roman Missal*, 70.

that designing banners can become a competition and become a distraction. (See the section on environment.)

Rehearsing and practicing for the liturgy:
Rehearsal is important but the extent of rehearsals depends on how formal the celebration will be. Everyone wants the liturgy to run smoothly and for the children to know what is expected of them. Yet if the children have been attending Mass regularly, they should already know what it is they need to do. Only a few things truly need to be rehearsed, such as processions.

In the end, the adults are the ones preparing the liturgy, and those adults should be well versed in liturgical practice.

5. What works best when teaching children how to receive Communion?

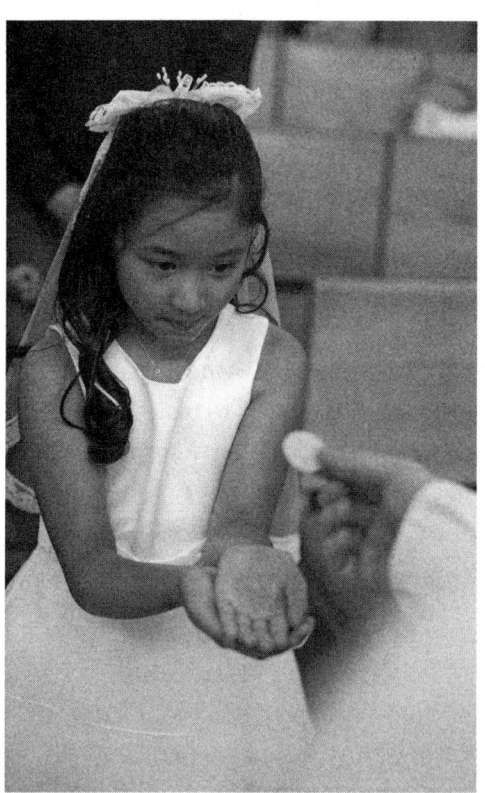

The child places their dominant hand under their other hand in order to receive Communion.

When catechizing, emphasize with the children that they are approaching the Table of the Lord. It is Christ that they are processing forward to receive and they must approach with reverence and an awareness of what they are doing. There are many practical issues that must be covered during the time of catechesis and formation to prepare children to receive Communion in an informed and reverent manner. While the children have often seen their parents, siblings, and other parishioners receiving Communion, they probably have not paid close attention to the actions involved. As a result, it is important to demonstrate to the children how to receive Communion and to actually practice receiving Communion. This can be easily done in the classroom with the catechist, and parents can be asked to practice at home using a small piece of bread.

It is best to avoid using candy or crackers, as the children should understand that the host is real bread that will become the Body of Christ when it is consecrated at Mass. While the bread they might practice with will be of a different consistency than the hosts used at Mass, it is a better substitute than crackers or other stand-ins. If possible, use real unconsecrated hosts for final rehearsal in order that the children will not be surprised on the day of First Communion. Remind the children of the difference between the unconsecrated hosts they are practicing with and the consecrated Body of Christ they will soon receive at Mass.

Most of the children in a parish will most likely receive on the hand unless that is not the parish's practice. It is not that simple however. Anyone who has distributed Communion, both clergy and extraordinary ministers of Holy Communion, has many anecdotes on the way they have experienced people receiving Communion. Some children, and adults as well, have the tendency to simply lift their palm to their mouth to consume the host, or move the host to the fingers on the same hand in which they receive it and then place the host in their mouth. Both these methods leave the host open to being dropped. It is one of the reasons practicing with the children is so important. After the child approaches the minister, he or she bows their head as a sign of reverence to Christ present in the Eucharist. After making the sign of reverence, the child places their dominant hand under their other hand in order to receive the Body of Christ. The upper hand should be cupped slightly. Instruct the children to raise their hands to at least chest height in order that the minister does not need to bend down to distribute Communion.

The next movement is a good option and also needs practice. After the child receives the host, they may take a step to the side, and taking their dominant hand, using the thumb and forefinger (and possibly the middle finger as well), they pick up the host gently, reverently, and carefully. Explain that they are not to bite off a piece of the host, but place the host as a whole in their mouth. Raising the palm to the mouth to receive the host, as if eating popcorn or candy, is to be avoided. The slow deliberate movement of taking the host in their fingers and placing it in their mouth again shows great reverence and creates an awareness of whom they are receiving. This is not just eating a piece of bread, but consuming the Body and Blood of Christ. Only when they have consumed the host are they to return to their seat.

In most parishes there are a good number of people who receive on the tongue, and perhaps there are a few parents who choose to have their children receive in this manner. The wishes of the parents should be respected in this regard. Be sure you are aware of those who desire this well before the date of First Communion, in order that these children will be able to practice receiving on the tongue. Although receiving on the tongue is the traditional way to receive, so often people who receive on the tongue today are not properly instructed how to do this. Many do not open their mouths wide enough, do not extend their tongue, or they may bite down on the host as the minister places it in their mouth. Any of these practices increase the chance of the sacred host falling, hence the practice of using a paten when Communion was only distributed this way. In fact some parishes still use a paten no matter how a person chooses to receive. It is important to practice if a child is going to receive in this manner. Some catechists might want to practice both ways with the children and let them, or their parents, make the choice.

Children should carefully take the cup from the minister with both hands.

The children who are receiving on the tongue should be taught to keep their hands folded as they approach the minister so that the minister knows they are receiving in this manner. After bowing their head, instruct the children to tilt their chin up a bit, open their mouth wide, and to extend their tongue. Tell them to picture the way they say "ahhh" at the doctors, but not to extend their tongue as far out. When the priest or minister places the host on their tongue, they bring their tongue back into their mouth and close their mouth. They do not need to step to the side when receiving on the tongue but simply return to their seat.

You will also need to practice with the wine. It's best to use the unconsecrated wine and the same vessels that will be used the day of celebration. Children should carefully take the cup from the minister with both hands and hold on to it firmly. Instruct them to take a small sip, or to simply touch their lips to it. They then return it to the minister, again with both hands. Instruct them not to let go of the cup until the minister has a firm grasp of it. If necessary, the minister can assist the child by holding on to the cup up to their lips. Some parents may wish that their children do not receive from the cup. This is acceptable; however, all should be catechized that receiving both species is a fuller expression of the Eucharistic mystery but that Christ's presence is found in both the consecrated host and the consecrated wine.

Children need to be catechized as to the fact that once they receive First Communion they are more active participants in the Eucharist in that they can receive Christ with others in the assembly every time they come to Mass. They also need to know that the manner of receiving Communion is either on the tongue or on the palm of the hand. Children should have the choice of how they wish to receive and that receiving the host requires that they know how to reverently receive. Although it may sound obvious and redundant, reminding children to always have clean hands when receiving Communion is necessary.

6. Are the children permitted to chew the host?

There is always a question as to whether or not chewing the host is allowed. While many older people were taught never to chew the host, there are no directives with regard to this practice. In John's account of the Gospel, Jesus tells the people, "Whoever eats my flesh and drinks my blood has eternal life" (John 6:54). The word "eats" is translated from the Greek *trōgō*, which means "to gnaw or chew." Some hosts, especially those made with whole wheat, are thicker than the commonly used thin white hosts. A small number of parishes bake their own bread, which is often thick and dense. These hosts do not easily dissolve, therefore some chewing is necessary. It is important to also remind the children not to chew the host with their mouth open, lest the host fall out, and never to remove the host from their mouth.

7. What if a child has difficulty swallowing the host?

On occasion, a child may have medical conditions in which they have difficulty swallowing. Parents should let the director of religious education or persons responsible for preparing children for the liturgy become aware of the situation. In cases such as this, the priest can be alerted to give the child a portion of the host instead of a whole one. Remember, Christ is present even in the smallest piece of the consecrated host.

8. What if a child does not like the taste of the host or wine, or refused to eat the host or drink from the cup?

Occasionally there is a child who will not want to receive the host or drink from the cup because of the taste or texture or on rare occasions has a psychological block with regard to eating the Body and Blood of Christ. This is why it is important to practice with unconsecrated hosts and wine beforehand in order that there are no "surprises" the morning of First Communion. As with those who have difficulty swallowing, a small piece of the host can be given to the child. If the child still refuses, it might indicate that the child is not yet ready to receive. No child should be forced to receive the Eucharist. It is important to work with the parents and the child to resolve these issues. We are not denying the child the sacrament but delaying reception until the child is truly ready to receive Communion.

9. Why can't a child with celiac disease or other form of gluten intolerance receive a host made of rice or other gluten-free substance?

The response to this question requires both pastoral sensitivity and a clear statement of the Church's teaching. Parents, children, family members, pastors, catechists, lay ecclesial ministers, and anyone else involved with a child who has celiac disease, gluten intolerance, or other allergies that prohibit him or her from receiving the wheat host consecrated as the Body of Christ or consuming the wine consecrated as the Precious Blood need to participate in open and honest discussions. These discussions provide the space for children and parents to name their feelings and concerns about the situation, as well as to ask questions. Mark your pastoral response with compassion. Anytime a child senses that he or she is different or will stand out among their peers, there is potential for the child's self-esteem to be negatively affected and the child to be marginalized. The child's reception of his or her First Communion is a sacred time. His or her experience of First Communion provides a significant perspective from which he or she will understand faith and the Church in the years ahead. The child and his or her family need to be treated with reverence and holiness; they are God's children. Every effort needs to be made to allow the child to participate fully in the Sacrament of the Eucharistic sacrifice and meal.

A clear statement of the Church's teaching includes the presentation of Canon 924 § 2, "The bread must be only wheat and recently made so that there is no danger of spoiling." This canon is the basis for the Church's teaching that the only valid matter to be transubstantiated into the presence of Christ's Body is wheat. The latest teaching on the Church's response to those with celiac disease comes from then Joseph Cardinal Ratzinger in 2003 when he was still Prefect for the Congregation for the Doctrine of Faith.[4] This teaching affirms that low-gluten hosts are valid matter for the celebration of the Eucharist, as is *mustum*, which is grape juice freshly made or preserved without altering its nature. The validity of *mustum* makes it possible for those who are unable to consume the Precious Blood in the form of wine. The Church does hold that hosts in which the gluten has been completely removed are invalid matter for the celebration of the Eucharist.

The Secretariat of Divine Worship of the United Catholic Conference of Bishops approves three distributors of low-gluten hosts for use in the United States.[5] For some children with celiac disease or other gluten intolerance, the low-gluten hosts from one or more of these distributors might be suitable. For others, whose doctors have advised them to avoid all gluten, even these low-gluten hosts will be unsuitable.

With the prevalence of celiac disease and other forms of gluten intolerance on the rise, your parish might already have a practice for pastorally responding to children and adults who are not able to consume the wheat host. This would be the place to start in presenting practical options for a child who is unable to receive the wheat host. If your parish makes low-gluten hosts available to people with celiac disease or other gluten intolerance, this is one option for the child. Make sure the low-gluten hosts are placed in a separate pyx and that precautions are taken to avoid contamination from the wheat hosts. The low-gluten hosts should be consecrated at the same time as the wheat hosts.

You will also want to speak with the celebrant and/or the extraordinary ministers of Holy Communion to alert them of the need to use low-gluten hosts. Also, consider where in the Communion procession the child(ren) who

---

4 See "Circular Letter to all Presidents of the Episcopal Conferences concerning the use of low-gluten altar breads and mustum as matter for the celebration of the Eucharist," accessed December 29, 2014, http:// www.vatican.va/roman_curia/congregations/cfaith/documents /rc_con _cfaith_doc_20030724 _pane-senza-glutine_en.html.

5 "Celiac Disease, Alcohol Intolerance, and the Church's Pastoral Response," accessed December 29, 2014, http://www.usccb.org/prayer-and-worship/the-mass/order-of-mass /liturgy-of-the-eucharist/celiac-disease-and-alcohol-intolerance.cfm.

need to receive the low-gluten hosts will be. Having the child(ren) be first or last in the procession could have the potential of drawing unnecessary attention to them. Weigh this possibility along with the practical need to identify the child(ren) who will need the low-gluten hosts—although the child(ren) or their parents will probably self-identify when they approach the priest or extraordinary minister. Inform the priest and/or the extraordinary ministers at which stations those who need low-gluten hosts will be receiving Communion.

If a child is unable to consume a low-gluten host because of his or her medical condition or high sensitivity to gluten, those responsible for the faith formation of the child and his or her family also need to communicate the Church's belief that Christ is fully present in both the consecrated bread and wine. This means that when a person partakes of the consecrated wine, he or she participates in the fullness of the Sacrament of the Eucharist; he or she fully receives the Lord. The same is true for a person who is unable to receive the Precious Blood. When he or she consumes the consecrated host, he or she fully receives the Lord.

If you determine that receiving the Precious Blood is the best option for the child, it will be important to understand your parish's practice regarding the breaking of the large host over the chalice and other Communion cups. If the host is only broken over the chalice, then make sure to have the child receive from one of the other Communion cups so as to prevent a reaction because of contamination. Also, if the child will only be receiving from the cup, you will want to communicate this to the pastor or the extraordinary minister who will be serving at the station the child will approach. This will help to prevent surprise reactions or judgments that the child could personalize in a negative way simply because of a lack of preparation and understanding on the part of others.

Other children and families might notice that a child or children are not receiving the host. While you do not want to discuss children's medical conditions with others, you will want to teach all the children in sacramental preparation sessions what it means to say the fullness of the sacrament is present in consecrated bread alone and the consecrated wine alone. Allow children and family members to ask questions about what this means and respond accordingly, without pointing out specific children.

Parish-wide education with regard to celiac disease and other gluten intolerances will help assist those involved in responding to children. Let parishioners know that low-gluten hosts are available, if this is a practice of your community. Advise parishioners on how and when to communicate with either the priest or extraordinary ministers of Holy Communion with regard to consecrating and receiving these hosts. Determine if there is a specific Communion station at which the low-gluten hosts will be available or if some will be available at each station. Parish-wide formation on this issue is also a form of pastoral outreach. Others in need of the low-gluten host might step forward because you have shown it is possible for them to receive the consecrated bread.

The last word that a child and family need to hear is that their child is a beloved child of God just as the children are who do not have celiac disease or forms of gluten intolerance. Within the bounds of Church teaching, you will want to provide for the needs of the child and his or her family so that he or she is able to celebrate the fullness of the Eucharist and experience the joy of knowing the grace of Christ in this sacrament!

10. Is it necessary to make the Sign of the Cross after receiving?

It was the tradition decades ago that upon receiving Communion the Sign of the Cross was made. There was no directive requiring this practice. It seemed to develop out of pious tradition. Many people still practice this today and children are still taught to bless themselves in a good number of parishes. The *General Instruction of the Roman Missal* does not specify any gestures that are to be made after consuming the host, and it has never been an official Church teaching to do so. It is customary in many places but would be considered a personal act of piety.

11. Can members of the parish community bake bread for the celebration of First Communion?

Church law is quite clear about the bread that is used for Mass. The bread

> "must be unleavened, purely of wheat, and recently made so that there is no danger of decomposition. It follows therefore that bread made from another substance, even if it is grain, or if it is mixed with another substance different from wheat to such an extent that it would not commonly be considered wheat bread, does not constitute valid matter for confecting the Sacrifice and the Eucharistic Sacrament. It is a grave abuse to introduce

other substances, such as fruit or sugar or honey, into the bread for confecting the Eucharist. Hosts should obviously be made by those who are not only distinguished by their integrity, but also skilled in making them and furnished with suitable tools."[6]

The *General Instruction of the Roman Missal* notes that "by reason of the sign, it is required that the material for the Eucharistic Celebration truly have the appearance of food."[7] Providing that only water and wheat flour is used and that the bread has the appearance of food, there is no reason that a parish could not bake bread for the celebration of the Eucharist. The Diocese of Davenport has prepared a resource with directions for how to make the Eucharistic bread including variations of the ratio of flour to water, cooking times and temperatures, and scoring directions. The resource may be found here: http://www.davenportdiocese.org/lit/liturgylibrary/Policies/litRecipes EucharisticBread-updated112711.pdf.

12. Is it permissible to have a private celebration of First Communion?

As mentioned previously, the Eucharist is a sacrament of unity, a parish event. For rare and exceptional cases, the pastor may allow a private celebration, but it should not simply be for the reason of convenience or wanting just family and friends to be present. Many times this request is because of very exceptional circumstances such as serious illness of the child or a family member. If there is a private celebration, it should be celebrated at a Mass in the church or a chapel. The celebration of Mass in a private home, catering hall, or outdoors is to be avoided.[8]

13. Do godparents have a role in the First Communion liturgy?

It is admirable to consider including the child's godparents in the liturgy. However, there is no ritual specifically for the godparents. This does not mean godparents cannot serve during the Mass. If a godparent is a trained liturgical minister in the parish where First Communion occurs, they might be considered to minister in some capacity, such as a reader, extraordinary

---

6   *Redemptionis sacramentum*, 48.
7   *General Instruction of the Roman Missal*, 321.
8   See *Redemptionis sacramentum*, 108.

minister of Holy Communion, or minister of hospitality. Godparents can also be asked to be part of the procession with the gifts. To ask all the godparents to be part of the liturgy might be difficult for many families. Godparents may have moved, passed away, or are no longer involved with the family. If a parish wanted to do something special with the godparents, they might schedule an evening of prayer for parents and godparents, keeping in mind that all the children's godparents might not be available.

14. Are children required to fast before receiving Communion?

The custom of fasting is ancient and found in almost all faith traditions as a means to attain holiness. It is "in keeping with the profound reverence which we owe to the supreme majesty of Jesus Christ when we are about to receive him hidden under the eucharistic veils. . . . Not only does this fast discharge the obligation of honor to the divine Redeemer, but it also fosters devotion."[9]

The requirement of fasting before receiving Communion has changed over the last century. The pre-Communion fast has gone from beginning at midnight, to three hours before receiving in 1953, to the current one hour established after the Second Vatican Council. This one-hour fast is not burdensome or difficult to do. The fast is required one hour before receiving Communion, not one hour before Mass begins. The symbolism of the fast is to make the recipient hungry for the Lord, to be nourished and filled by his Body and Blood as real food for the salvation of our souls.

When catechizing children about fasting, we need to present it as a good thing and not as a burden. Given that a normal Sunday Mass usually lasts between fifty minutes and a little over an hour, if something is eaten before leaving home for Mass, it will most likely be over an hour before Communion is received. The fast is from all food and drink. Water and medicines are exempt. Consuming food during the hour because of medical conditions is always permissible.

Many times parents bring food into church to keep babies and toddlers quiet. By the time a child reaches beyond toddler years this should be unnecessary. It is also a temptation to older children and even adults to eat some of the toddler's food that is brought into church. When parents make

---

9   Pope Pius XII, *Christus Dominus* (January 1953), in the *Liturgy Documents: Foundational Documents on the Origins and Implementation of Sacrosanctum Concilium: Volume 3* (Chicago: LTP, 2013), p. 186.

sure children have eaten a good breakfast before coming to church, children will not be looking for something to eat. Soft toys and books instead of food keep toddlers occupied and quiet and do not tempt older children and adults to help themselves to the toddlers' snack. While some might argue that chewing gum does not break the fast since it is not swallowed, it is quite inappropriate to be chewing gum in church.

15. What happens if a child does not want to celebrate the Sacrament of Reconciliation?

There can be a variety of reasons why some children are afraid to go to confession. Most of the time, celebrating the sacrament out in the open instead of inside a Reconciliation room relieves fears. Sometimes having a priest sit down with the child and his or her parents, and having a casual conversation about what happens when going to confession, helps the child understand that nothing bad is going to happen. The parents can then leave the room and the priest can hear the child's confession. Priests can be very pastoral in dealing with these situations. If it is noticed beforehand that a child might have problems celebrating this sacrament, or if the parent mentions it, speak to the priest about it. Ensuring the child is well prepared and knows exactly what to expect is one of the best ways to avoid any anxieties about celebrating Reconciliation.

16. Our parish has made changes to the way we celebrate First Communion. A few parents are upset with the changes. How do we help them understand the parish's rationale for the changes?

The "we have always done it this way" mentality is a difficult one to overcome, and there will no doubt be some hurt feelings or even anger over any major changes to the First Communion liturgy. Often, many of the things being changed have nothing at all to do with the reception of Communion, but deal with externals, such as having the children stand in the sanctuary to sing a song, placing banners on the pews, presenting flowers to Mary, or a myriad of other innovations that have crept in over the years. Older siblings might have celebrated Communion in a certain way and parents want their younger children to experience the exact same things.

People do not like change, especially if they feel that something does not need changing. The pastor, priests, catechetical leader, and those preparing the liturgy must be very considerate of the parents' feelings. It is important to convey the reasons honestly but with authority. It is best not to spring changes to the celebration last minute. Introduce the fact that changes are being made at the first parent meeting or in a letter at the beginning of the year. Listen attentively to the objections and avoid being defensive. If possible meet with those who are upset and let them know they are being heard. State the reasons for the decision and be able to back it up with documentation if possible. Always assure them that the celebration will be beautiful and meaningful without the things that are changing or being left out. This is a catechetical moment when you can help parents to gain a greater appreciation of the beauty of the Order of Mass, without add-ons. Remember we cannot please everyone, and for each person who objects, there are many, many more that may like the changes, but remain silent. As Pope Francis says, "Pastoral ministry in a missionary key seeks to abandon the complacent attitude that says: 'We have always done it this way.' I invite everyone to be bold and creative in this task of rethinking the goals, structures, style and methods of evangelization in their respective communities."[10]

---

10 *Evangelii gaudium*, 33.

APPENDIX I:
The Sacrament of Reconciliation

Preparing Children to Celebrate Reconciliation

The *National Directory of Catechesis* notes that, in addition to being prepared to receive the Eucharist, children are to be well prepared for the Sacrament of Reconciliation.[1] The Church requires that children celebrate this sacrament before receiving First Communion. Reconciliation is a sacrament that has seen a dramatic decrease in its reception since the 1970s, and there are many thoughts as to why this has occurred. Since many parents do not celebrate the sacrament it is important that priests, liturgists, and catechists portray the sacrament in a very good light and encourage parents, as well as the children to celebrate Reconciliation.

It is important when catechizing about Reconciliation to draw upon their experiences of forgiving and being forgiven. Children at this age need to know that just as their parents forgive them for wrongs they might do, so too will God forgive them for the things they do that are wrong. We should not be afraid to use the word "sin," but it is also important to help the children know the difference between committing a deliberate sin as opposed to doing something wrong by accident. A good example that explains this would be spilling a glass of milk accidently as opposed to throwing a glass of milk on the floor out of anger. Children of this age are still learning right from wrong and discussing situations and having them decide if it is right or wrong helps them to understand the difference. Some catechists develop games to help children learn the difference between sins and accidents, or that help children identify sins that they might commit.

The most important concept that they need to understand is that Reconciliation brings them into a right relationship with Christ. It renews a

---

[1] See *National Directory for Catechesis*, chap. 36, sect. A, 3a, and chap. 36, sect. B, 2.

friendship with Christ that gets hurt when they commit wrongs on purpose. It is the same thing as when they do something wrong to a friend or when a friend hurts them in some way. Their friendship is hurt and may be broken. When forgiveness is sought and accepted, the friendship heals and becomes whole again. Explain to the children that the same thing happens when they commit sin. After committing sin, their friendship with Christ needs healing. Help them to know that when they confess their sins to the priest, it is not the priest they are speaking to but Christ. Also it is Christ who is forgiving them when the priest says the prayers of absolution. Children also need to be assured that the priest cannot tell anyone, not even mom and dad, whatever the child tells the priest in confession. This reassures the child and helps them to speak honestly with the priest. Parents need to know that they should not tell the child what to confess or question the child about what it was they said to the priest.

Going through the Rite of Penance several times, as it will be celebrated in your parish, will help children become more comfortable. Be sure to find out what the confessor will expect of children. Some may expect a conversation which they will lead, others may expect children to name one or two sins. This is also an area of preparation for parents and children to work on together. Seeing and hearing others go to confession is better than making something up. Of course don't let the children confess their real sins. Catechists could give the children one or two "sins" to say when they practice. Having a priest come in to talk to the children about Reconciliation and what they should expect also helps them prepare to make their confession. The priest can even demonstrate with a mock confession. If the children become familiar with the parish priests by asking them to come to class sessions or greet them in the halls before and after class, they will be more comfortable confessing to the priests.

The Rite of Penance

The ritual used is the *Rite of Penance*. There are three forms of celebrating the sacrament. The first option is the "Rite for Reconciliation of Individual Penitents."[2] This is the most common option, where the penitent goes to the church at times scheduled for confession, enters the confessional or Reconciliation room, and celebrates the sacrament in private. The penitent

---

2   See *Rite of Penance*, 41–47.

has the option of confessing face to face or behind a screen. The second option is celebrating the sacrament as part of a Reconciliation service, better known as the "Rite of Reconciliation of Several Penitents with Individual Confession and Absolution."[3] In this form a large group can celebrate the sacrament at the same time as part of a community. Additional priests can be brought in to help hear confessions if the group is large. The third form is the "Rite for Reconciliation of Several Penitents with General Confession and Absolution," which is absolution without individual confession, and is only to be celebrated in extreme and rare situations.[4]

Many parishes hold a Reconciliation service (the second option of the rite) the first time the children go to confession. This is the form that many schools and religious education programs use for those children receiving for the first time. A Reconciliation service is a liturgy of the Church and needs to be prepared well in advance of the service. The second option includes an Introductory Rite, a celebration of the Liturgy of the Word, the Rite of Reconciliation, and a Concluding Rite. Liturgical ministers should be scheduled to greet the assembly and hand out worship aids (if used), proclaim the readings, cantor, and provide additional music.

Music is an important part of the Reconciliation service. An opening hymn should be selected to gather the community of children and adults as the priest enters the church and processes to the sanctuary. A Responsorial Psalm is sung as well as a Gospel acclamation if a Gospel is proclaimed. Hymns can also be sung during the time that individual confessions are happening. These can be sung by the entire assembly or interspersed with solo or instrumental pieces. A congregational song for the praise of God's mercy is also to be sung when all have participated in confession and have returned to conclude the service. Live music is always preferred.

The Introductory Rite is similar to the Introductory Rite at Mass except that there is no Gloria and no Penitential Act since the Rite of Penance will be celebrated. The priest welcomes those gathered and says some words of introduction and perhaps some instruction as to what is happening. Finally there is a Collect, or opening prayer.[5]

The Liturgy of the Word is then celebrated. It can be a full Liturgy of the Word with two readings, a Responsorial Psalm, and a Gospel; however

---

3 See *Rite of Penance*, 48–59.
4 See *Rite of Penance*, 60–66.
5 The Introductory Rite is found in the *Rite of Penance* at articles 48-50.

you might choose to do one reading, a psalm, and a Gospel, or simply a reading and a Gospel. The readings are found in the *Rite of Penance* or in the *Lectionary for Mass*.[6] Children usually like the story of the Lost Sheep and this is a popular one for children's first celebration of Reconciliation. Following the readings there is a brief homily focusing on the love and mercy of God. The children (and their parents) can also be reassured that this is a sacrament of Christ's love that prepares them to receive Christ in Communion. The priest might want to say something to the parents as well, as a number of them might have been away from the sacrament for a while. It helps tremendously if the parents have a positive attitude about going to confessions and celebrate Reconciliation at the same service as their children. An examination of conscience follows the homily. It usually takes the form of a litany, for example: "For the times when I have not been nice to others, Lord have mercy," with all repeating, "Lord, have mercy." This may be read by the priest, a deacon, or another reader. Don't make it too long, just focus on some of the sins that young children might commit.

After the examination of conscience, the Rite of Reconciliation begins.[7] First the priest or deacon invites all to make a general confession of sins. It may be the Confiteor, a penitential litany, or a penitential song. The Our Father and a concluding prayer follow. Then individual confession and absolution occurs. It is good for the presiding priest to introduce the other priests that will be present and to let everyone know where they will be stationed throughout the church. Many parishes celebrate First Reconciliation in the open instead of inside the Reconciliation room. This alleviates any fears a child might have and it makes the parents comfortable to be able to see their children. However be cautious that placement of these stations are such that confessions cannot be overheard. It is good to station catechists or other adults to help guide the children and keep any lines in order. The rite does not end with individual confessions. After each confession, the child returns to the main assembly. After all have finished, a song of praise for God's mercy is sung and a prayer of thanksgiving is said by all.

The Reconciliation service ends with a Concluding Rite.[8] This includes a simple blessing and dismissal. It would be appropriate to end with a final song.

---

6   See the Lectionary, #892–896, and *Rite of Penance*, 51-53.
7   See the *Rite of Penance*, 54–57.
8   See the *Rite of Penance*, 58–59.

A word of caution is needed with regard to First Reconciliation services. There is the danger that Reconciliation will turn into another moment that focuses more on the children rather than what the children are experiencing in the sacrament. The same problems that crept into First Communion celebrations are slowly finding their way into some Reconciliation services. Parents take videos and pictures of their children in what is supposed to be a very private and intimate encounter between the priest and penitent. Any photos can be taken following the service but never as the children are sitting with the priest. Elements such as lighting candles, dropping written sins into a pail or shredding them are often seen in books or articles about creative Penance services, yet as with First Communion, the symbol of the sacrament itself should be what stands out. Those who prepare Reconciliation services should follow the rite as provided in the *Rite of Penance*. Any innovative additions have the danger of taking the focus off of the actual celebration of the sacrament. Many children find the sacrament to be a very good experience without any extras added to it. If you feel you must do something, perhaps hand children a holy card or other symbol recognizing the celebration after the service is over. Children should also be encouraged to celebrate it frequently and even be encouraged to celebrate it again before they receive First Communion and regularly after that.

Parents too should be encouraged to celebrate the sacrament. A good number of parents might not have celebrated Reconciliation for many years, or since they were in religious education classes. Catechesis for this sacrament is probably more important for parents since their attitudes toward Reconciliation will pass down to their children. If parents do not see celebrating Reconciliation as important, the children most likely will not. When conducting parent meetings, it is good to encourage parents to celebrate Reconciliation. Be available to discuss concerns they might have with regard to issues in their lives that keep them from this healing encounter with Christ. Many parents have come back to the Church because of caring priests, catechetical leaders, and catechists who gently and compassionately listened to their fears, their pain, their difficulties, and helped them to return to the sacraments. It is a good idea to have some written resources available to give to parents that explain Reconciliation.

APPENDIX II:
Other Ritual Experiences for Children

> Children are to continue to be instructed through catechetical instruction and formation after the reception of First Communion.
>
> —*Code of Canon Law*, 777 §3

Parish Liturgy

There is no better way to prepare children to receive First Communion than by having them participate in the parish's celebration of the Eucharist at Sunday Mass. "In the Church's mission of evangelization, catechesis and Liturgy are intimately connected."[1] The Church's liturgy catechizes the faithful through words and music, through sight and smells, through touch and taste. The symbols of the liturgy speak when there are no words to express what is being experienced. Through rituals that have developed and evolved over millennia, Catholics have come to grow in their relationship with the Lord, with the Church and with each other.

Unfortunately, in today's society symbols don't speak to people as they once did. We need to introduce children to the symbols used in the liturgy. This can be done in the classroom or at home. Catechists and parents can make use of holy water and candles (with great caution). Gestures that are used in the liturgy can be used during prayer time. While it might be impractical to have children kneel in class for prayer, certainly standing tall with their hands folded would be helpful in keeping their focus and in understanding that this is something special. When they see the priest and others using these gestures at Mass, they make the connection with what they did in class or at home. Sometimes, instead of using traditional prayers (Our Father, Hail Mary) or prayers that are found in the textbooks or from other sources, use

---

1 *National Directory for Catechesis*, 33.

the prayers of the liturgy to open and close class sessions. These prayers can be found in liturgical books, but many monthly publications that people use at Mass provide the daily prayer texts. The children might not understand all these prayers, but they will get used to hearing them. When you are reading Scripture in class, read it in the context of a prayer service, using a modified Liturgy of the Word ritual. When praying intercessions in class, follow the format for the Universal Prayer at Mass and have the children respond as they would at Mass.

Pay attention to the liturgical year, the seasons and feasts that we celebrate as Catholics. Help the children to identify the colors associated with each season and what they mean. As the seasons change, ask the children what they noticed different in the church that signals a change of season.

It is always good to bring the children to the church during class times or at special sessions with parents for prayer, or to go over the parts of the Mass. Some parishes even celebrate an instructional mass at which time they go through each part of the mass as if it were really being celebrated. The priest or a commentator would stop at the different parts and explain what is happening. There can be time for questions following the presentation. Tours of the church are another way to help children become engaged in the liturgy. As they learn to recognize the signs and symbols, movements, gestures, words, and songs of the liturgy, the liturgy will come alive for them.

Participation at Sunday Mass is the best way to form children in the faith.

Prayer

Prayer is communication with God. It is talking and listening to God who is the center of our lives and whom we are called to love above all things. When we are in a loving relationship with someone, we engage in conversation with them, sharing our thoughts, our hopes, our dreams, our pain and sorrows, our disappointments, and our joy. We listen to what they have to communicate to us. A relationship devoid of communication, of talking and listening, is bound to falter. The same is true with our communication with God. In order to foster a loving and living relationship with God, we all need to take time to speak to the Lord in prayer.

The family is the first place where prayer is learned and experienced. "For young children in particular, daily family prayer is the first witness of the Church's living memory as awakened patiently by the Holy Spirit."[2] Parents can begin to introduce the practice of prayer by praying with their children at bedtime and at meals. Bedtime prayer becomes such a cherished time that children will remind parents when it is forgotten. Many children have been lulled off to sleep after reciting the prayer to the Guardian Angels or while praying a family Rosary.

In addition to learning the basic prayers such as the Hail Mary and the Our Father, children can pray for people in need. This is the beginning of learning to pray intercessory prayer. Children can and do make very profound prayer requests, along with praying for pets and lost objects. Praying at meals, as explained previously, helps children to understand that we receive all things from God and he deserves our thanks and praise. Children can also be encouraged to pray to God in their own words and to speak to God during the day. So many young children have imaginary friends that they speak to; why not encourage them to speak to God who is very real and very present to them at all times. Parents sometimes talk about how they overhear their children talking to God at night, and when parents pray, they often notice their children imitating them. The old saying, "a family that prays together stays together," rings true, and we live in a time where family prayer is so much needed.

Regrettably many families do not pray together, nor do parents teach their children to pray. A guest speaker was asked to speak to a group of children preparing for First Communion. She asked the students who first taught

---

2   *Catechism of the Catholic Church*, 2685.

them to pray. Expecting the students to say that their parents taught them, she was taken back when one student raised his hand stating that Mrs. Grant, his catechist of many years, taught him to pray. The presenter was probably a bit naïve expecting that parents are always the ones who introduce prayer to their children. Catechists often are dismayed that many children in their classes do not know basic Catholic prayers. They do not know how to make the Sign of the Cross or even understand what prayer is. This is why it is so important that catechists pray with the children in their classroom. Prayer needs to be a part of every catechetical session. Children who have learned to pray find it comforting and familiar, and once they begin formal catechesis and formation they often volunteer to help lead the class in prayer and intercession. At this age, children are comfortable praying in front of others and that should be encouraged. Time should be spent helping children learn to pray together and alone. If children can easily memorize songs, poems, and jingles, they can certainly memorize prayers. Parents every so often say that they begin to pray with their children after the children come home from class and ask their parents to pray at meals or at bedtime. Children often bring their parents back to an active faith. Catechists can ask the parents of children in their class to help the children learn the prayers. Younger children are so happy when they come to class and report that their parents prayed with them and that they know their prayers. Pastors or catechetical leaders should always pray with parents at the beginning of meetings and gatherings. Some parents may feel uncomfortable at first, but so often they come to appreciate it. When meeting with parents individually, it would also be good to start or end with a prayer, especially if parents are going through a difficult time. This would also be a good time to encourage them to pray with and for their children. Prayer is very powerful.

Silence

Silence is another form of prayer that is important for children who in today's world are bombarded with noise throughout the day, as well as distractions from TV, video games, and even the Internet at this young age. Teaching children that sitting quietly and simply thinking about God is an excellent form of prayer and helps them to listen to what God is saying to them in their heart. Catechists can lead children in guided meditations. They love when the lights are dimmed and they take that quiet time to focus on words that both teach them about God and lead them closer to God. It is prayer using their imagination, and we all know that children have great imaginations. Tap into that imagination in the form of prayer. Parents and catechists can ask the children about their prayer and what they heard God saying to them. Asking children to write their own prayers is another way to encourage them to communicate with God. Some catechists have the children keep a prayer journal using words and pictures to record their prayer experiences. This will help them be comfortable with liturgical silences.

Scripture

The Scriptures are not just ancient stories in a book that we keep on a shelf in our homes. The Scriptures are the Word of God. They are our story, the story of who we are as followers of Christ. They are the history of our salvation. Beginning at the creation and continuing with the revelation of God to the patriarchs, the Scriptures are the story of God's covenant with the Hebrew people, the story of the Jewish people and their breaking and renewal of the covenant, and the story of reconciliation with God. The New Testament leads us through the coming of Christ, his life, his teachings, his Death, Resurrection, and Ascension, and ending with the story of the early Church. The Scriptures teach us about Christ and how to be Christians. The Scriptures we hear at Mass on Sunday also go beyond just stories of our faith, they help us to be prepared to receive Christ in the Eucharist.[3] It is through Scripture that we learn the history of salvation and the path to eternal life. But it is more than that; it is God speaking to us. The proclamation of Scripture is one of the modes of the presence of Christ during the celebration of the Mass.

For many Catholics, Sunday Mass is the only time they are exposed to Scripture, but the hearing of Scripture should not be limited to Sunday Mass. Children, as well as adults, benefit greatly from reading the Bible at home. Reading and reflecting on the Sunday readings before attending Mass helps adults and children to not only become more familiar with the Scriptures, but also helps them to apply the Scriptures to their lives. Sharing the Scriptures beforehand also helps the children to pay better attention when hearing both the readings and the homily at Mass, as they recognize what is being read.

A good children's Bible is a wise investment as children are able to read the Scriptures on their own. Make sure it is a Catholic edition or that it

---

3   See *General Directory for Catechesis*, 70.

contains the deuterocanonical or apocryphal texts, that is those books left out of Protestant editions of the Bible. There are also resources both in print and online that assist parents and catechists to explore the Scriptures with children. Taking advantage of these resources assists parents and catechists in making the Scriptures come alive, but make sure that the resources contain nothing opposed to Catholic teaching.

Fostering a love of Scripture helps children to come to know Jesus and to understand our Catholic faith. Parents can read a passage to their children before bedtime, or take out time during the week to read the Sunday Scriptures and talk about them. Catechists, along with parents, can teach the children how to look up passages in the Bible. Ask children to tell a Bible story in their own words, memorize a line from the Sunday Scripture, or draw a picture of the Bible story. Catechists should incorporate the Sunday readings into their lesson plan. Some passages may be difficult for children to comprehend. A good commentary helps parents to understand passages and explain to their children what the passage is about. There are also many games, puzzles, coloring, and activity sheets available online to help children to understand the readings.

After attending Mass, parents can talk about what the priest or deacon said in the homily. What words, stories, or ideas did the children hear in the homily? How will what was said in the homily help them to follow Jesus? The ride home from Mass or time spent at the family dinner table are great times to talk about what was heard in church that day. It is also beneficial for catechists to take time during class to explore these same questions with the children. Relate the Scriptures to real life and they will come alive.

Pastors, liturgists, and catechetical leaders can offer Bible study or Scripture sharing groups for parents and other adults to help them grow in love of the Scriptures. Open all parent meetings with Scripture and allow time for participants to reflect upon the Word of God. Questions about the Sunday readings, for both adults and children, can be printed in the bulletin each week as conversation starters. In class, ask the children what they heard in the Scriptures. The more you as catechists, pastors, and parents expose children to the Scriptures, the more they will understand what it means to be a Christian and to grow in their relationship with God.

Blessings

"*Blessing* expresses the basic movement of Christian prayer: it is an encounter between God and man."[4] Blessings can be a divine action of God, a free gift from the Lord, or it can refer to our offering praise and adoration to God. In the literal sense from the Latin word *benedicere*, "to bless" means "to speak well of." When a blessing is given to someone, God is asked to look kindly upon a person, to pour his grace upon them, and they in turn are called to thank the Lord for the blessing. Blessings are important because they help us to recognize and acknowledge that God is acting in our lives.

One does not need to be a member of the clergy to bless someone. We do it all the time when we say "God bless you" when someone sneezes. Grace before meals is a blessing when we thank God for our food. Parents can be encouraged to bless their children often and indeed many parents do bless their children before they fall off to sleep or head out the door for school. It can be as simple as asking God to bless them, or by making the sign of the cross on their heads. Many parishes invite parents to bring home holy water on the day of their child's Baptism and to use it to bless their children. It can be easily replenished at any church or a priest or deacon can bless plain water at any time.

Blessings can be used for various occasions in the home and family. *Catholic Household Blessings & Prayers* includes many blessings that can be used at home for things like blessing a home, blessings for a new job, the beginning of the school year, the blessing of a Christmas tree, and so much more. Many include readings from Scripture and can be prepared so that different people in the family can take part. This resource includes a blessing of a child before receiving First Communion that can be prayed by family members.

During their time of preparation for First Communion there can be many opportunities for the children to receive blessings in the parish. Just as the period of the catechumenate contains formal blessings for those preparing for their initiation into the Church, blessings can be given to children at various times during their time of preparation for First Communion. Catechists can bless the children as they enter or leave the class or a blessing can be part of a classroom prayer service. These blessing rituals also help the children take part in the Mass, since many of these blessing can occur within

---

4 *Catechism of the Catholic Church*, 2626.

a word service, similar to the Liturgy of the Word at Mass. The children can be blessed at Mass when they begin their preparation for First Communion. Chapter 5 in the *Book of Blessings* includes the "Order for the Blessing of Students and Teachers." This blessing might be appropriately used at Mass by the priest celebrant or deacon to bless children as they begin their preparation. The ritual provides intercessions that may be incorporated into the Universal Prayer. The prayer of blessing concludes the Universal Prayer. The order of blessing may also be done outside of Mass by a catechist.[5] If so the "Order of Blessing within a Celebration of the Word of God" is used. The *Book of Blessings* also includes the "Orders for the Blessings that Pertain to Catechesis and to Communal Prayer" of which the Order of Blessing for a Catechetical or Prayer Meeting would be appropriate (chapter 4). Pastors might consider using the "Order for the Blessing of Rosaries and the Order for the Blessing and Conferral of a Scapular" if these gifts were given to first communicants. The blessing of religious articles such as rosaries and scapulars must be done by the priest or deacon.

Mystagogical Formation

We see it too often in our parishes where First Communion is such a special day but then we do not see the children and their families the next Sunday or for weeks or months following their First Communion. It might help to provide opportunities for families to gather together on Sundays both at Mass and after Mass. The children and their parents have gone through a preparation period yet it seems like after First Communion they are simply let go until the next catechetical year begins. If we view First Communion as a time when we are not only preparing children but evangelizing families, then the time after First Communion is an opportune time to continue evangelizing through well-prepared experiences of Church through liturgies and other parish activities that draw families into the life of the parish.

Mystagogy is a term used in the *Rite of Christian Initiation of Adults* for the period following initiation. It basically means to break open the mysteries. It is a time when the newly initiated explore what they experienced at the Easter Vigil and delve deeper into what it means to be a Catholic Christian.

---

5   Laypersons may preside over certain blessings. However, note the rubrics in the Book of Blessings. Certain gestures and texts are reserved to the priest and deacon and alternate gestures are provided for the lay minister. For example, a priest or deacon prays with arms outstretched while a lay minister prays with hands joined.

Following First Communion there are different ways to plan mystagogical experiences for the children and their families that focus on what the children experienced at their First Communion and what it means for them as they grow in their faith. Catechists, pastors, and liturgy and music directors can collaborate on these ideas together:

- Ask the children to wear their First Communion outfits to Mass in the weeks following their First Communion. They serve as a witness to the community in the same way neophytes (those initiated at the Easter Vigil) give witness to their conversion by wearing their white garments to Mass. This also reminds the children that every time they receive Communion it is special. Acknowledging the presence of the children at Mass the weeks after First Communion encourages them and makes them feel like they are a welcomed part of the community, which they are.

- The parish can host a "Communion Breakfast" one Sunday for all the children who have just received First Communion and their families. Have a guest speaker, one who can engage both the children and the parents about the Eucharist. Ask a family to give a brief "witness talk" about their experience of preparing for and receiving First Communion. This would be a good time to have the children sing a special song or for the pastor to present them their First Communion certificates.

- Plan a May Crowning. Decades ago this was an annual event at most parishes. May is a month when the Blessed Mother is honored in a special way. At this parish celebration, the first communicants carry flowers and gather around a statue of the Blessed Mother. They lead those gathered in a Marian song, perhaps pray a decade of the Rosary or another prayer, and then one child is chosen to place a crown of flowers on the statue. This can happen following a Sunday Mass or at a prayer service on a Saturday morning. Next year's First Communion class can prepare refreshments to follow the May Crowning.

- On the Solemnity of the Most Holy Body and Blood of Christ (*Corpus Christi*), which acknowledges Catholic belief in the present of Christ in the Eucharist, the Mass is followed with a Eucharistic procession. The Blessed Sacrament is placed in a monstrance and processed through the church, the streets, or around the outside of the church. The priest carries the monstrance and a baldachin (a canopy) is held over him and the monstrance. The assembly follows in silence or sings Eucharistic songs. Invite the children, dressed in their Communion outfits, to take part in the procession as a group. They can carry flowers or drop petals in front of the priest carrying the monstrance. The procession ends at a prepared station where Benediction is celebrated. This experience helps reinforce in the children and their families the Catholic devotion to the Eucharist and the Real Presence of Christ.

- Plan occasional gatherings for families after Mass. These can be simple opportunities for refreshments and hospitality, or more organized sessions where there is a specific program for children and adults, such as intergenerational catechesis, or separate programs for the children in one room and the adults in another. Any opportunity to gather together can be mystagogical. These opportunities are not just for recent first communicants but for all families.

RESOURCES

Ritual Texts

It is important for those preparing liturgies for First Communion to have access to the liturgical books that are used in the Church's liturgies and sacramental celebrations. They are available from various publishers. Liturgy Training Publications offers study editions for the Order of Mass and the *Lectionary for Mass.*

- *The Roman Missal*
- *Lectionary for Mass*
    Volume I: Sundays, Solemnities, and Feasts of the Lord and the Saints
    Volume II: Weekdays Year I
    Volume III: Weekdays Year II
    Volume IV: Ritual and Votive Masses
- *Rite of Penance*
- *Rite of Christian Initiation of Adults* (see part 2, section 1: Christian Initiation of Children Who Have Reached Catechetical Age)
- *Book of Blessings*
- *Catholic Household Blessings & Prayers*

Liturgy Preparation Resources

- Driscoll, Michael S., and J. Michael Joncas. *The Order of Mass: A Roman Missal Study Edition and Workbook.* Chicago, IL: Liturgy Training Publications, 2011. Designed as a workbook, this resource provides an overview of the rubrics for Mass while offering theological insights about the various texts and prayers.
- Lewinski, Ron. *Making Parish Policies: A Workbook on Sacramental Policies.* Chicago, IL: Liturgy Training Publications, 1996. This workbook will help a parish review its sacramental and liturgical

practices and consider what kind of policies may be helpful for the community. Exercises present a method for addressing issues and developing policies.

- *The Liturgy Documents, Volume One: Fifth Edition* and *Volume Two: Second Edition.* Chicago, IL: Liturgy Training Publications, 2012. Included in these volumes are the essential documents needed for those involved in liturgy preparation. See especially the *Constitution of the Sacred Liturgy, General Instruction of the Roman Missal, Sing to the Lord: Music in Divine Worship, Redemptionis Sacramentum, Built of Living Stones, Guidelines for the Celebration of the Sacraments with Persons with Disabilities,* and the *Directory for Masses with Children.*

- *National Directory for Catechesis.* Washington, DC: United States Conference of Catholic Bishops, 2005. This document explores the role of the catechesis and provides information regarding the sacramental preparation of children.

- Piercy, Robert Jr. *Preparing Masses with Children: 15 Easy Steps.* Chicago, IL: Liturgy Training Publications, 2012. Piercy not only goes over each aspect of the liturgy, but also offers suggestions for including students in preparation for liturgies. It is appropriate for both parish school and religious education programs and is a good resource for parish liturgy committees as well. Included in this volume is a sample preparation guide.

- Turner, Paul. *Ages of Initiation.* Collegeville, MN: The Liturgical Press, 2001. This brief volume explores the Sacraments of Initiation from the first century to current times. It contains a good explanation of the evolution of First Communion for children at the age of discretion. It also explores the restored order of the Sacraments of Initiation for children.

- Turner, Paul. *At the Supper of the Lamb: A Pastoral and Theological Commentary on the Mass.* Chicago, IL: Liturgy Training Publications, 2011. This book is both a commentary and a study guide. It includes insightful and challenging discussion questions that can be used not only with those preparing the liturgy, but with catechists and parents as well. It includes texts from the revised translation of *The Roman Missal.*

- Turner, Paul. *Let Us Pray: A Guide to the Rubrics of Sunday Mass.* Collegeville, MN: The Liturgical Press, 2012. Contained in this volume is a guide and commentary to the rubrics of *The Roman Missal* regarding the celebration of the Mass. It is extremely helpful to presiders and to those preparing the liturgy.
- Various authors. *Sourcebook for Sundays, Seasons, and Weekdays.* Chicago, IL: Liturgy Training Publications, published annually. Provides valuable insights for preparing liturgies and the sacramental rites.

Low-Gluten Hosts

Low-gluten hosts are approved for use by the USCCB for persons with gluten intolerance or celiac disease. These hosts contain the minimum amount of gluten acceptable for valid matter for the Eucharist and are deemed safe for those suffering from the disease. The use of these hosts should be discussed with a physician before use.

The following distributers produce low-gluten hosts approved by the USCCB Secretariat for Divine Worship:

- Benedictine Sisters of Perpetual Adoration
  31970 State Hwy, Clyde, MO 64432-8100
  Phone: 800-223-2772
  Website: www.benedictinesisters.org
- Parish Crossroads
  P.O. Box 2413, Kokomo, IN 46904
  Phone: 800-510-8842,
  Website: www.ParishCrossroads.com
- Additional distributor for Parish Crossroads:
  CM Almy
  28 Kaysal Court Armonk, NY 10504
  Phone: 800-225-2569
  Website: www.Almy.com
- GlutenFreeHosts.com, Inc.
  100 Buckley Road, Liverpool, NY 13088
  Phone: 800-668-7324, ext. 1
  Website: www.GlutenFreeHosts.com

Diocesan Guidelines

Below are web addresses to a select number of diocesan guidelines for preparation for First Communion and First Penance. These guidelines were established for specific dioceses to be used by their parishes and apply only to their diocese. However those preparing guidelines for dioceses and parishes can use them as a guide in preparing their own. It is important for parishes to check with your diocesan Office of Worship or Faith Formation Office before promulgating your own guidelines as your diocese may have specific mandates.

- Diocese of Fort Worth, TX
  http://www.fwdioc.org/files/sacramental_guidelines_eucharist.pdf
- Diocese of Fairbanks, AK
  http://dioceseoffairbanks.org/joomla/images/ministry/sacramental_preparation/sacramental_preparation_first_eucharist.pdf
- Diocese of San Jose, CA
  http://www.dsj.org/wp-content/uploads/2013/05/Eucharist.pdf
- Diocese of Gallup, TX
  http://www.dioceseofgallup.org/Documents%20and%20Forms/Sacraments/EUCHARIST.pdf

GLOSSARY

Alb: A long, white garment, worn by priests, deacons, and by lay ministers as well. It is a reminder of the white garment given in Baptism.

Ambo: The place from which all the Scripture readings are proclaimed and the homily may be preached during liturgy; a pulpit.

Apostles' Creed: The ancient baptismal statement of the Church's faith. The questions used in the celebration of Baptism correspond to the statements of the Apostles' Creed. It may be used as the Profession of Faith at Mass, and is particularly appropriate during Lent, Easter Time, and during children's Masses.

Blessed Sacrament: The name commonly used to refer to the Eucharistic elements of bread and wine after they have been consecrated and have become the Body and Blood of Christ. The term may also be used to refer to the consecrated bread alone.

Celiac Disease: Those affected with this disease cannot ingest gluten from wheat without becoming ill.

Chalice: The sacred cup used to hold the wine which becomes the Blood of Christ at Mass. It is sometimes called a "Communion cup."

Ciborium (Ciboria): The sacred vessel, usually with a cover, that holds the hosts for the distribution of Communion and to store the consecrated hosts in the tabernacle. These vessels are usually either bowl- or chalice-like in shape. They are usually made from metal and should be unbreakable.

Code of Canon Law: The collection of laws for the Roman Catholic Church.

Communicant: Any person who receives Communion.

Communion Rail: The railing found at the edge of the sanctuary in some churches at which communicants would kneel while receiving Communion.

Communion Rite: The last part of the Liturgy of the Eucharist. It begins with the Lord's Prayer, and includes the Sign of Peace, the Lamb of God, during which the fraction of the host takes place, and distribution of Holy Communion. The Communion Rite ends with the Prayer after Communion.

Concluding Rites: The last part of the Mass, following the Communion Rite. It begins immediately after the Prayer after Communion and consists of brief announcements, a greeting, blessing, and the dismissal of the assembly.

Consecrated: Refers to the bread and wine that have become the Body and Blood of Christ during Mass (see consecration below).

Consecration: The part of the Mass in which the priest prays the words of Jesus at the Last Supper over the bread and wine. The bread and wine cease to be bread and wine (although the appearance of bread and wine remain); they become the Body and Blood of Christ.

Corporal: The square, white linen cloth placed on top of the altar cloth upon which any chalices and ciboria are placed during the celebration of Mass. Any vessels (chalice, ciborium) holding the Blessed Sacrament are to be placed on the corporal.

Credence Table: A table in the sanctuary on which the wine and water cruets, water basin/pitcher, and towel are placed for the celebration of the Mass.

Epiclesis: The part of the Eucharistic Prayer in which the priest invokes the Holy Spirit so that the gifts of bread and wine will be transformed into the Body and Blood of Christ and that there will be unity among the members of the assembly who partake of the Body and Blood of Christ.

Eucharistic Prayer: The "center and high point of the entire celebration."[1] It begins with the Preface dialogue and continues with the Amen as a single prayer.

Eucharistic Species: The consecrated Body and Blood of Christ. Also called the sacred species.

Extraordinary Minister of Holy Communion: A nonordained person who is deputed to distribute the Body and Blood of Christ for either a single Mass or on multiple occasions.

---

1 *General Instruction of the Roman Missal*, 78.

Form: The text or formula that forms the verbal aspect of a sacrament. Form is frequently linked to matter in a description of a sacramental rite. The form of the Eucharist has traditionally been seen as the words of Christ within the Eucharistic Prayer, the Institution narrative.

General Instruction of the Roman Missal: The primary document that provides specifics for celebrating the Mass.

Host: The traditional name for the circular unleavened wafer of bread used at the Eucharist in Western churches. It derives from the Latin *hostia*, meaning "sacrificial victim." The *General Instruction of the Roman Missal* urges the use of a host large enough to be fractioned and shared by the priest and at least some of the people.[2] When used in the plural as in "God of hosts" or "heavenly hosts" the word refers to angels (from the Latin *hostis*, "army").

Institution Narrative: The section of the Eucharistic Prayer in which the presiding priest narrates what the Lord Jesus did and said at the Last Supper when he instituted the Eucharist. The traditional Catholic teaching has been that when the priest repeats the words of Christ during this section of the Eucharistic Prayer, the bread and wine are consecrated and become the Body and Blood of Christ. Thus the Institution narrative is sometimes also referred to as the Words of Institution or the Consecration.

Intercessions: Refers to appeals or requests on behalf of others, such as mediation. In this sense, we ask others, including Christ, his mother, the angels, saints, and the People of God to intercede for us through their prayers and merits.

Intinction: A method of receiving Communion in which the priest dips the consecrated host into the Precious Blood, says "The Body and Blood of Christ," and places it directly on the tongue of the communicant. Only a priest or a bishop may distribute Communion in this manner.

Introductory Rites: The first part of the Mass. It includes the entrance song, procession, veneration of the altar, Sign of the Cross, Greeting, Penitential Act, Sprinkling Rite, Gloria, and the Collect.

Lectionary for Mass: The series of ritual books that contain the readings used during Mass.

Lectionary for Masses with Children: The ritual books including readings that have been adapted for the liturgical and cognitive needs of children.

---

2   *General Instruction of the Roman Missal*, 321.

Liturgy: From a Greek word *leitourgia*, which means "work of the people," it can refer to any official form of public worship. In the Eastern Churches, the Mass is often called the Divine Liturgy. The title is frequently used in conjunction with a modifier, such as the Liturgy of the Hours, the Liturgy of the Word, Liturgy of the Eucharist, etc., although it is not uncommon in popular parlance for people to use the phrase "the liturgy" to refer to the entire Mass.

Liturgy of the Eucharist: Follows the Liturgy of the Word, beginning with the Preparation of the Altar and the Gifts, and includes the Eucharistic Prayer, Communion Rite, and Prayer after Communion.

Liturgy of the Word: The term for the section of the Mass that follows the Introductory Rites and ends with the Universal Prayer. It consists of several readings from Scripture, followed by a homily, the Profession of Faith (if prescribed), and the Universal Prayer. On Sundays and other important celebrations, three readings are used; on weekdays, only two. On Sundays and Solemnities, the readings follow this order: First Reading (usually from the Old Testament), the Responsorial Psalm, the Second Reading (a reading from one of the New Testament Epistles or from Revelation), the Alleluia or Verse before the Gospel, and then the Gospel.

Lord's Supper: A name taken from 1 Corinthians 11:20, sometimes used for the Mass, to emphasize its connection to the Last Supper. It is used on Thursday of Holy Week (Holy Thursday), when the principal liturgy is called the evening Mass of the Lord's Supper.

Matter: The physical material and the gestures that together form the major visible aspect of a sacrament. Matter is frequently linked to form in describing a sacramental rite. The matter of the Eucharist is the wheat bread and grape wine.

Mystagogy: A time for the newly-initiated to unpack the meaning of the sacramental mysteries that have been received and to become more deeply immersed in the life of the Church.

Paten: The name for the plate used to hold the Eucharistic bread. Although the term is especially associated with the small plate used to hold the host for the priest, it can also be applied to a larger plate containing a sufficient number of hosts for the communion of the entire assembly. May also refer to the plate held underneath the ciborium while people are receiving Communion.

Penance: An act imposed on the penitent by the priest as part of the Sacrament of Penance. It is meant to be a remedy for sin and a help in changing one's life, and should include remedy for any injury done to others, if appropriate. The penance imposed should in some way correspond to the sin and might take the form of prayer, self-denial, or some work of service or mercy toward another person. Also a popular way of referring to the entire ritual of the Sacrament of Penance.

Piety: "Public or private expressions" of the Christian faith that are "not part of the liturgy."[3]

Pyx: A small round vessel, often shaped like a pocket watch, in which the consecrated host is carried to the sick, homebound, and dying.

Ritual: A name given to any formalized action. Normally, it refers to special religious activities that have a set structure and order and employ religious symbols and texts. In general, however, "ritual" can refer to any human activity that marks significant moments through expected and repeated patterns of behavior or rules of actions. Examples of secular rituals include folk dancing, sports customs (e.g., the seventh-inning stretch), and birthday traditions. Both secular and religious rituals include rules (or rubrics), repeated behavior by key "celebrants," and expectations by the "assembly." Ritual creates and establishes a common identity and a shared perspective of reality.

Ritual Mass: In *The Roman Missal*, a category of Mass formularies to be used when sacraments and other rituals are celebrated within Mass. Examples include Masses for the Conferral of the Sacraments of Initiation, for the Conferral of the Anointing of the Sick, for the Conferral of Holy Orders, and for the Celebration of Marriage.

The Roman Missal: Formerly called *The Sacramentary*, it is the liturgical book that contains the rubrics and prayers for the celebration of the Mass according to the Roman Rite.

Sacrament: In the most general definition, a "sacrament" is a visible sign of an invisible grace.

Sacrament Chapel: A separate place for the reservation of the Eucharist (consecrated bread) in the tabernacle.

---

3 *Directory on Popular Piety and the Liturgy*, 7.

Sacrifice: A means by which human beings offer reverence to and establish communion with God. The Mass is a sacrifice in that it makes present the ultimate sacrifice of Jesus on the Cross. We unite ourselves to Jesus' sacrifice through the prayers, hymns, and lives of the assembly.

Sanctuary: The area of the church in which the presidential chair, altar, and ambo are located, and in which the primary ministers may also sit. Normally it is somewhat elevated, for the sake of visibility. It should be in some way distinct from the other areas of the church, yet at the same time integrally related to the entire space so as to convey a sense of unity and wholeness. It is sometimes referred to as the presbyterium or chancel.

Spiritual Communion: Uniting oneself to Christ and to the Christian community through prayer. This is often practiced by those who are not able to receive Communion.

Tabernacle: The safe-like receptacle for storing the consecrated Eucharistic bread, the Body of Christ (the Precious Blood is not reserved in the tabernacle). The tabernacle must always be locked while the consecrated hosts are stored in it, and a burning candle or oil lamp (the sanctuary light) should be nearby. The tabernacle must be immovable, solid, and not transparent.

Transubstantiation: The term given to the traditional Catholic theological explanation regarding the change of the bread and wine into the Body and Blood of Christ during the celebration of the Eucharist. The term is based on the belief that the substance of the bread and wine is changed, but the external accidents (appearance, taste, etc.) remain unchanged.

Votive Mass: A Mass celebrated at the discretion of the presiding priest. The texts used are not those of the liturgical season or day, but are taken from a selection of Masses honoring God, Mary, the angels, or the saints. Liturgical norms regulate when Votive Masses may and may not be used.